COMMUNION

AN INTIMATE STUDY OF PRAYER

BY ROBERT L. MARTIN

Communion: An Intimate Study of Prayer
By Robert L. Martin © Copyright 2020
All rights reserved.

All Scripture quotations, unless otherwise noted, are taken from the Holy Bible, King James Version (Public Domain).

All Greek and Hebrew translations are taken from the New Strong's Exhaustive Concordance of the Bible, James Strong, Copyright © 1990 by Thomas Nelson Publishers. All Greek and Hebrew words are italicized. Used by permission. All rights reserved.

Visit God's Word Prevails for more books, articles and inspiration at GodsWordPrevails.org

ISBN: 978-0-9993062-1-5

Cover and Book Design by Exodus Design Studio
www.ExodusDesign.com

Printed in the United States of America

DEDICATION

To the Glory of God our Father,
Jesus Christ our Saviour,
And Holy Spirit our Counselor

It is with humble gratitude that I present this work for your glory, Oh Lord Most High. You are the One who deserves all honor and glory for the wisdom given within the pages of this book. My prayer is that all who read this will be strengthened and encouraged through the precious Words you pour forth through this journey of Communion. Heavenly Father manifest yourself to every person who steps through the doors of this book. This I ask in the precious Holy Name of Jesus Christ.

TABLE OF CONTENTS

ACKNOWLEDGMENTS

Let me take a moment to share my gratitude with those who inspired me to take up the journey and write this book.

First, my Lord Jesus - I love you, Lord! The words within these pages were only made possible by you! I could do nothing at all, were it not for the presence of the Holy Spirit. Thank you, my Lord, for all you have given me. I am truly humbled to see the richness which you brought forth. It is truly your work! Now I present it back to you for your Glory!

To my beloved Paula - I can't begin to express the thanks I have for your loving support and input. God has given me great insight through you, and I thank Him every day for your selfless love to me. Thank you for taking the time to pray with me, encourage, and help me along this journey of ours. My beloved, you are precious to me beyond words! I love you, my Gorgeous! May our Lord Jesus continue filling you with His love, strength, joy, and peace as we walk together on our journey.

My dear departed friend - Pastor Luis Cuebas - who taught me that battles are won in the prayer arena! I thank God for the love you gave and the wisdom you imparted. I will always treasure the precious moments we shared.

To my dear sister in Christ - Marilia Cuebas - Thank you for all the encouragement through the years and for being a true friend to Paula and me. Your prayers have been effectual, and we have been undergirded by them often. May our Lord reward you greatly for your sacrificial offerings on our behalf. You are greatly loved my wonderful sister in Christ!

To all who have been an influence in my life to follow Christ - May God richly bless you according to His loving kindnesses and tender mercies.

PREFACE

The purpose of any study is that one would become knowledgeable and skillful in that particular field. In other words, a person doesn't just seek to know but seeks to become skillful in the exercise of this wisdom. If all one does is learn without growing in the practical use of knowledge it would be a waste of the valuable time each person is given.

The reason for writing this book is that those who read it may grow in the knowledge and understanding of our Blessed Heavenly Father and our Lord Jesus Christ. It is also that each one might become skillful in the practical use of this wisdom. My prayer is that we will grow in Christ Jesus and become fruitful branches for His glory and to His praise!

The subject we will endeavor to examine is Prayer! It is with this precious instrument of grace that each key point will be investigated. It is with prayer that we will become knowledgeable and skillful in its practical application daily. And, it is through prayer (communion) that our eyes will begin to see the glory of our God manifest through our lives.

Prayerfully consider the time you give to the reading of this book. I believe in doing so, it will be a great key that can be used throughout your journey of life. It is my hope, through these pages, that we can behold together what God reveals to us and grow thereby. I humbly commit these words to our Lord Jesus Christ and seek His counsel through the Holy Spirit!

INTRODUCTION

Prayer is the door through which we enter into the presence of The Living God. It is holy communion with our Heavenly Father and our Lord Jesus Christ. Prayer is the means by which we understand the heart of our Lord, and it is never one-sided. There are many forms of prayer, but all effectual prayers are through our Great Intercessor! This door is Jesus Christ, our Lord. He is the Great Intercessor, who is ever interceding for His beloved ones. So then, Christ is the door through which we come into the presence of our Heavenly Father. Holy and heartfelt prayers bring us into agreement with Him! Through our standing in agreement with Jesus, the prayers we offer will be effectual because they become One with Christ, who is The Truth!

As we begin our journey, let us put aside any preconceived ideas about this subject and humbly seek the face of Jesus Christ for a fresh understanding and anointing to walk out what He reveals to us.

Father God, we come to seek your face, and as we prepare, grant us wisdom and grace to know and understand your ways. Impart unto us your Holy Spirit as we seek to know you more and grant us your favor in Jesus' Holy Name, I ask! Amen!

We will undoubtedly find many great nuggets of truth along this journey, and I do not know how long we will linger in this pasture. However, it matters not how long we tarry; it matters that we grow in the knowledge of our Heavenly Father, of His Son Jesus Christ and His ways!

Enter with me now as we contemplate *"Communion - An Intimate Study on Prayer."* May the Spirit of The Living God guide us as we humbly seek His Face! Amen.

CHAPTER 1
The Purpose of Prayer

What is the primary *"Purpose of Prayer"*? As I have been carefully contemplating the answer to this question, the Holy Spirit revealed some things to me, which I had not understood before. He posed this question to me and then began to stir my heart with the answer. The Holy Spirit directed me to look at the passages of Scripture found in Matthew and Luke, where Jesus teaches the disciples to pray.

I believe it is important to note, before we lay the foundation, that prayer without studying the Word of God is fruitless. If we would know the will of God, it is through prayerful study of His Word. We pray for counsel, read the Scriptures, pray for wisdom and understanding, then, listen for our Lord's counsel.

It is written: *"Ask, and it shall be given you; seek, and ye shall find; knock, and it shall be opened unto you: for everyone that asketh receiveth; and he that seeketh findeth; and to him that knocketh it shall be opened"* (Matthew 7:7-8).

Asking is approaching our Father in heaven through prayer. Seeking is the searching out of the Scriptures with an expectation that our Lord will reveal Himself to us as we search. Knocking is continuing to come in spite of the obstacles in our way, trying to hinder us from finding the will of God in a particular situation.

The words used in the previous text I quoted imply continuance in our asking, seeking, and knocking. With this in mind, let's consider the prayer our Lord Jesus taught.

The Scriptures are found in Matthew 6:8-15 and in Luke 11:1-4. We will examine the verses found in Matthew because this prayer is like the one Jesus gives His disciples in the book of Luke. Matthew 6:8-15 reads:

> *v8 Be not ye therefore like unto them: for your Father knoweth what things ye have need of, before ye ask him.*
>
> *v9 After this manner therefore pray ye: Our Father which art in heaven, Hallowed be thy name.*
>
> *v10 Thy kingdom come. Thy will be done in earth, as it is in heaven.*
>
> *v11 Give us this day our daily bread.*
>
> *v12 And forgive us our debts, as we forgive our debtors.*
>
> *v13 And lead us not into temptation, but deliver us from evil: For thine is the kingdom, and the power, and the glory, for ever. Amen.*
>
> *v14 For if ye forgive men their trespasses, your heavenly Father will also forgive you:*
>
> *v15 But if ye forgive not men their trespasses, neither will your Father forgive your trespasses.*

Jesus says, *"After this manner pray ye."* This being the model for prayer, which our Lord taught the disciples, it must also be the primary purpose for all prayer.

Communion is enriched with God through prayer. And, it is through our communion with God that we participate in establishing His Kingdom and His will on the earth and in our lives. These are not self-centered prayers seeking only for what we want, but rather, prayers that stand in agreement with our

Heavenly Father and with our Lord Jesus Christ. Were the Lord to have instructed His disciples to pray for any other thing, the focus would've been different. So, by this, we know the primary *"Purpose of Prayer."*

There are several things to reflect upon in this prayer. Consider the following:

- Bread given

- Mercy extended

- Keeping and Deliverance offered

Here in this passage of Scripture, the outline of what the will of our Heavenly Father is for the Kingdom becomes evident. *"On earth as it is in heaven..."* We commune with God for our daily bread. This request is in agreement with the will of Father God. For, there is an abundance of bread in our Father's House, and He gives us instruction to ask for this bread to be released to the hungry. So we pray; Let there be abundance in Your House, Oh Lord, here on earth as it is in heaven, the Bread of Life for the hungry, the Water of Life for the thirsty, the Oil of Joy for the weary. We pray for provision to be released to and throughout the Body of Christ that all who are hungry and thirsty might find sustenance. To reiterate, the prayer is not a selfish one, which should be understood because it is written with a focus on family; *"Our Father who art in heaven..."*. It is plural, not singular, though He is my Heavenly Father. Yes, we can ask for God to supply our personal needs but, shouldn't we ask Him to provide for us that which is lacking so we may, through His gracious provision, advance His Kingdom too? I believe this should be the case.

Jesus taught us that our Father knows what we need before we ask. However, He instructs us to seek first the Kingdom of God, revealing another confirmation that the primary *"Purpose of Prayer,"* which is communion with God, is to establish His Kingdom!

Notice carefully that I said our prayers are communion with Father God and His Son Jesus Christ. Prayer is never one-sided! It is the joining of our heart to His and His heart to ours, becoming one. We come into agreement with God as we learn to hear His voice through prayer. It isn't just asking and hoping He will answer. Rather, it is the key to breaking through into intimacy with God!

Prevailing prayers are those that move us into deeper fellowship, where we hear and see what our Heavenly Father is doing. Once we reach this place, we join our hearts with His and speak what He has spoken in order to establish His Kingdom and will in the earth, *"as it is in heaven."*

Consider the second segment of this prayer, and we behold mercy offered. Our Heavenly Father extends mercy to us through His Beloved Holy Child Jesus Christ, and through our communion with God, mercy is obtained for ourselves and those who sinned against us. Mercy was freely given to us when we were in our worst state. So, as we present petitions before our Heavenly Father to forgive us, we remember the great offenses God has cleansed us from and plead with Him to release His Mercy to the persons who may have wronged us too.

The Mercy of The Lord endures forever, and since this is part of His nature, which God revealed through the offering of His Son, we likewise offer Mercy to others. *"...Freely you have received, freely give"* (Matthew 10:8). It is our Father's will that not one perish. So, our prayer must agree with His will and through communion with Him, we release His Mercies in the earth and in the midst of the Body of Christ.

Again, prayer moves us into unity, oneness with our Heavenly Father, that the rich mercies of our gracious Lord Jesus may be abundantly given to His beloved people. As we pray, in this manner, our Father in heaven bountifully grants us His mercies!

It is written, *"Blessed are the merciful, for they shall obtain mercy"* (Matthew 5:7).

I believe it is very important to place emphasis on Matthew 6:14-15 as part of Christ's teaching on prayer because verse 14 begins with the word *"for"*:

> *v14 For if ye forgive men their trespasses, your heavenly Father will also forgive you:*

> *v15 But if ye forgive not men their trespasses, neither will your Father forgive your trespasses.*

This is key to being positioned to receive an answer from Father God! If we don't extend mercy to others, how can we expect our Father in heaven to honor our petitions? Jesus made it clear by what He taught that God expects us to forgive if we would have forgiveness. This is why it is included at the end of this prayer. I believe it is placed here, so we might understand as well that communion with our Heavenly Father is from a heart of mercy! (Side note; examine Micah 6:8 to understand more clearly what God requires regarding mercy.)

Next, we petition our Father for His Keeping and Deliverance. There are a vast number of things in this world that attempt to divert our attention. However, if we run headlong into them, without communing with our Lord Jesus about the problems at hand, we can become ensnared. Temptations are on every side, but God has promised to be our Guide. Even so, it is important to ask for His keeping and deliverance, according to His Counsel!

Drawing near to God is through obedience before Him that we might obtain the promise of His keeping. We agree with our Father in heaven regarding His Kingdom and ask for deliverance to be released on the earth and in His household. All this we do that our Father in heaven might be glorified. *"For, Thine is the Kingdom, and the Power, and the Glory, for ever. Amen."*

Notice the progression of this prayer. First, we seek the glorious Kingdom of our God and Father to be established according to His will, as it is in heaven. This is righteousness, peace, and joy in the Holy Ghost, which directs us to bread, The Bread of Life! Second, we ask for this Bread. Jesus Christ is that Bread which came down from heaven (John 6:32-42). He is Bread indeed, and through Jesus Christ, we are enriched to know and understand God's plan for our salvation! As we begin to understand our Father's plan, it gives us boldness to ask for mercy. Third, moving forward yet once more, we ask our Father in heaven to forgive us of our sins. The Light of God's glory and grace was manifest as we received His Son, the True Bread. The Lord Jesus made known to us the will of our Heavenly Father, and we are compelled to pray accordingly by His Love! Father God sent His Holy Son that we might have eternal life through Him. He is the Bread of heaven, which gave His life for the world. May the Lord grant you to know and understand this is personal redemption! God didn't want to save some, but all! Our prayers once more unite our hearts with the will of our Father in heaven. We move out of selfish prayer into selfless prayer that others may also obtain like mercies. Thus, we beseech God's keeping and deliverance. Fourth, we ask our Heavenly Father for His mercies to continue, according to His will, by keeping us from besetting temptations and for His mighty deliverance when we find ourselves encountering evil. This brings our hearts to a place of worship, causing us to glorify our Father in heaven. For He is worthy of all glory, honor, and praise. God gave us Life and Victory through His Son, and this is His will! Let us then rejoice with the saints and angels above for our Heavenly Father's wonderful work of love and grace to us. Amen.

I believe there is a parallel of this prayer found in one of my favorite passages of Scripture from the Old Testament. It is Numbers 6:22-27 which says:

v22 And the Lord spake unto Moses, saying,

v23 Speak unto Aaron and unto his sons, saying, On this wise ye shall bless the children of Israel, saying unto them,

v24 The Lord bless thee, and keep thee:

v25 The Lord make his face shine upon thee, and be gracious unto thee:

v26 The Lord lift up his countenance upon thee, and give thee peace.

v27 And they shall put my name upon the children of Israel; and I will bless them.

The Priests were given this blessing to speak over the children of Israel. Notice it wasn't a selfish prayer but one which sought the benefit of The Lord God over all His people.

There is also a progression to this prayer, and it is a prayer of agreement with the will of God! The Lord commanded the Priests to bless His people in this manner, and He would bless them. Let's look at this! Remember, Our Heavenly Father, The Almighty God, The Lord Jehovah is the One to whom we bring our petitions.

Verse 24: "*The Lord bless thee, and keep thee...*" parallels the petition for our daily bread! The blessings of The Lord and His keeping speak of His watchful provision over our lives daily. He gives us manna from heaven, the Bread of Life, the Living Word of God, which is the true bread.

Verse 25: "*The Lord make His face to shine upon thee, and be gracious unto thee...*" parallels His merciful kindness to us. He makes His face to shine upon us that we may no longer be blinded by sin. God is then gracious unto us, mercifully forgiving our sins. We ought to do likewise. This is what Jesus teaches us through the prayer in Matthew.

Verse 26: "*The Lord lift up His countenance upon thee, and give thee peace...*" This speaks of the manner in which He guides us. We petition our God to lead us not into temptation, and here we see by His loving countenance the path is illuminated before us, and through His Holy Peace we behold His deliverance from every evil scheme of our enemy!

Verse 27: *"And they shall put my name upon the children of Israel; and I will bless them!"* Look at what The Lord God says! You shall put my Name upon them, invoke my blessings, in this way, and I WILL BLESS! The Lord God, our Heavenly Father, the One who is unchangeable, made this Holy Promise that He Will bless if we ask Him to do so, according to His will!

I believe there is so much more we can meditate upon within this verse. However, this is a summary of the primary *"Purpose of Prayer."* We commune with God The Father, God The Son and God The Holy Ghost through prayer and worship. By each of these methods, we seek to establish the Kingdom of our Lord and of His Christ!

Our hearts through prayer become united with our Heavenly Father, and by faith in God's promise, we establish His Kingdom. The Lord opens our eyes to see what He is doing through the Holy Spirit, and with the key *of "All Prayer,"* we proclaim our Lord's will in the earth.

One of the Keys to the Kingdom of Heaven is *"All Prayer"* (Ephesians 6:18). Paul speaks of this as he encourages his beloved brothers and sisters to *"put on the whole armour of God"* in his letter to the Ephesians. Verse 17 of Ephesians Chapter 6 ends with a colon, which is an extremely important part of the sentence structure. For, it reveals that the weapon of *"All Prayer"* is part of the armor we have been given to defeat the enemy of our souls. In Matthew 16:19, Jesus tells Peter He would give unto him, and us, the *"keys of the kingdom of heaven."* With these keys, things are bound in earth and heaven, and things are also loosed!

It is of great importance we learn to exercise this blessed key of prayer that the Word of our Lord Jesus, the Sword of the Spirit, the Twoedged Sword of Revelation 1:16, may also be in our mouths.

John Bunyan talks about this weapon of all prayer, in *The Pilgrim's Progress*[1], helping Christian overcome. In one place, it was the key to his deliverance from doubting castle, and, in another, it helped him combat the terrors he faced in the dark.

It is written; *"the Kingdom of God is not meat and drink; but righteousness, and peace, and joy in the Holy Ghost"* (Romans 14:17). Jesus spoke of the Kingdom of God saying: *"The kingdom of God cometh not with observation: Neither shall they say, Lo here! or, lo there! for, behold, the kingdom of God is within you"* (Luke 17:20-21). This reveals that the Kingdom of God isn't manifest with outward observances. It is established by the working of the Holy Ghost within our hearts and through communion with God in prayer.

Paul speaking to the Corinthians says, *"...the Kingdom of God is not in word, but in power"* (1Corinthians 4:20), signifying it is through the Holy Ghost that the Kingdom of God is manifest. The unity of the Body of Christ in the Holy Ghost establishes the Kingdom of our Lord and of His Christ, which is by prayer!

This is God's desire since it was what our Lord Jesus preached saying; *"The time is fulfilled, and the kingdom of God is at hand: repent ye, and believe the gospel"* (Mark 1:15), and again Jesus spoke saying; *"...I must preach the Kingdom of God to other cities also: for therefore am I sent"* (Luke 4:43). The Gospel of Jesus Christ declares the Kingdom of God, and this is the very thing we seek to establish in the earth through our prayers.

What other instances in Scripture can you find that reveal to us the primary *"Purpose of Prayer"*? I'm very confident that further studying will reveal many such passages of Scripture. Let's

---

[1] *The Pilgrim's Progress by John Bunyan, Published 1678*

continue to be prayerful regarding our study, and we will gain a great understanding of *"The Purpose of Prayer,"* which directs us right into *"The Power of Prayer."*

CHAPTER 2
The Power of Prayer

We've examined the *"Purpose of Prayer"* and found it is so we might establish the Kingdom of our Lord and of His Christ in the earth as we commune with Him! The effectiveness of prayer was revealed in action through our Lord Jesus Christ as we studied the prayer our Lord taught. This being the case, we should realize the Power our Lord Jesus gave us through this example.

The *"Power of Prayer"* is what we will contemplate now while recalling the *"Key of All Prayer."* Read the following Scriptures and think about them for a while. Luke 18:1-8 is a parable given to the disciples and recorded for our admonition. It reveals the necessity of faithfully praying. The parable also demonstrates the will of God and the power of praying persistently.

Remember, we are establishing the Kingdom of our God and His will in the earth! So, let's examine this passage and see what The Holy Spirit reveals to us.

Thank you, Heavenly Father, for the Living Word! Thank you for our Lord Jesus Christ and the blessed Holy Spirit whom you sent to us that we might know you and your blessed Son! Open our eyes and our ears, Lord. Grant us your holy Wisdom as we come to the Light of this Word you spoke so long ago. Your *Words are Spirit, and they are Life*, I thank you for them right now! Release your Holy Spirit in our midst in the lovely Name of Jesus Christ, our Lord! AMEN.

The parable our Lord Jesus taught from Luke 18:1-8 reads:

v1 And he spake a parable unto them to this end, that men ought always to pray, and not to faint;

v2 Saying, There was in a city a judge, which feared not God, neither regarded man:

v3 And there was a widow in that city; and she came unto him, saying, Avenge me of mine adversary.

v4 And he would not for a while: but afterward he said within himself, Though I fear not God, nor regard man;

v5 Yet because this widow troubleth me, I will avenge her, lest by her continual coming she weary me.

v6 And the Lord said, Hear what the unjust judge saith.

v7 And shall not God avenge his own elect, which cry day and night unto him, though he bear long with them?

v8 I tell you that he will avenge them speedily. Nevertheless when the Son of man cometh, shall he find faith on the earth?

To truly understand the Word our Lord Jesus speaks is first to recognize the One who is declaring it. Though some might say this was Luke, he was penning the very Words of our Lord Jesus as given by the ones who had been with Him! We recognize and believe these Words are from the lips of our Lord and, He instructed us according to the will of our Heavenly Father! In other words, The Father's Words were through Him (Jesus), to us!

Next, we should perceive why He gave this parable. The evidence is here for us to see, though we often overlook much of what was written for our admonition. Why was it documented? The very first verse answers this question so that we could understand our Lord's teaching. It was; *"To this end..."*. Now, some say this phrase was added to the original text so that we might read it more clearly. However, examining the next part of this verse, which reads; *"that men ought always to pray, and not faint,"* we can know with certainty that our Lord's purpose was for us to *"always pray, and not faint."* There is no need to question what Jesus was conveying.

Finally, we should realize that Jesus didn't just give us good suggestions, but *Word with Promise!* This is always present when our Lord speaks! He gives us *"Word with Promise,"* which will be a theme present throughout this study. Likewise, Jesus always gives us *Word with Power*, the very thing we are considering at present.

Verse 1 reveals Jesus wanted us to know, perceive, and understand; that men *"ought always to pray, and not faint."* What does the word *"ought"* mean? Looking closely at the Greek definition, we see it means a necessity, binding!

See the Greek according to the *Strong's Concordance* below:

> NT:1163 dei (die); third person singular active present of NT:1210; also deon (deh-on'); neuter active participle of the same; both used impersonally; it is (was, etc.) necessary (as binding):

> KJV - behoove, be meet, must (needs), (be) need (-ful), ought, should.

Notice the words don't read, *"it might be a good idea."* Rather, this is necessary for us! Examine other words derived from the Greek here, and they all reveal the will of our Lord. It was an urgent plea, not a calm suggestion that we pray always. Why? Well, the answer may be that when we are facing trials, which seem difficult to bear, our hearts faint within us.

Please understand, not only did Jesus urge us to pray but, He also said don't faint in the trial *while* you're praying. To faint is to lose heart, to become discouraged, afraid, weary or tired. There may be times in our lives when the battle continues to rage on, and we see no end in sight. This is the time we need to press in all the more. Our Lord Jesus wants us to get hold of this truth. There is power in persistent prayer, as we will soon see.

I believe it is important to recall that prayer is communion with our Heavenly Father and our Lord Jesus Christ! It is also defined as supplication and worship to God. To make earnest supplication and worship before our God is prayer. We may praise, sing a song, entreat God with groans, and great sighs, which are also forms of prayer. However, our communion should be in earnest, knowing that He is God and rewards those who diligently seek Him (Hebrews 11:6), with the understanding that He is our loving Heavenly Father. We can boldly come through Christ Jesus, our Lord, before our Father, who will not deny us access. The proof of access is in the very fact that He gave us His Son so that we would have this privilege. Praise His Holy Name!

Now, consider the parable carefully! What can we understand about the *"Power of Prayer"*? There is effectiveness through fervent prayer. The Scripture confirming this is: *"the effectual fervent prayer of a righteous man availeth much"* (James 5:16). We can see an example here of fervency, not letting go of God. It is a prayer that moves us *out* of our faithless selves *into* the faithful God. I say this because, many times, we are so overcome by circumstances our eyes cannot behold God. However, there is an assurance from Jesus Christ that He will hear and answer our prayer! So, we press in for victory; first, for victory over unbelief, then, for victory over our adversary!

It is important to understand that prayers are effectual as we set our gaze firmly upon Jesus. He is the Great Intercessor, and, as we fix our eyes upon Him, our hearts become ignited with His passion for the very thing we are seeking Him about.

Too often, we are like Peter, who walked upon the sea to our

Lord Jesus. He started well. But soon, Peter heard the winds and saw the waves around him roaring. It was then he began to sink. The sights and sounds caused him to doubt and so to sink. The good news is, he cried out for Jesus to save him, and our Lord heard his cry, raising Peter up. The wonderful thing about it is he walked back or was carried back to the boat with Jesus Himself. So, even if we stumble, we have a Rock that cannot be shaken. That Rock is Christ Jesus, our Lord. He will pull us through!

The saints of days gone by used to say, *"I prayed through."* I heard this often growing up, and I never quite understood what they were saying. However, I believe it means to pray until we see and hear the Lord's Word about the situations we are facing, by faith. Peter began to sink because of unbelief. We know this because Jesus asks him why he doubted (Matthew 14:31). So, praying through is praying until we break through in faith about the circumstance at hand. Why? The answer is: we can't receive if we do not believe that Jesus can or will do what we are requesting. Furthermore, I believe praying through is even deeper than this. It is quieting everything until you behold Jesus Christ as Lord and Saviour in and over it. This is often a difficult task, and the flesh will not want to do this. But, it is possible to get there, and I believe that is what praying through means!

Jesus promises us that God will respond to our fervent prayers, though Father God *"bears long"* with us. We have the assurance from our Lord that He will do so. I believe the reason this is true is that, when we beseech our God in prayer, we join with our Great Intercessor, who stands with us. We enter into agreement with God's will through Christ, who is right there petitioning our Father along with us!

As I write this, I continue to remind myself why it was written and who spoke these words.

Moving on, we see this widow woman was unjustly treated by

an adversary. They were trying to take what was rightfully hers and doing so by unjust means. Note also that her petition was before an unjust judge. What can we perceive from this? We live in the midst of a crooked and perverse generation, which know not God, nor do they care for His ways. Look at it this way; "*Get what you want, how you want, by any means you want, as long as you get what you want.*" As unjust as it sounds, this was the very thing taking place. We do not know what this adversary was trying to take. But, we know that our enemy, Satan, comes to steal, kill, and destroy (John 10:10). This is what was happening in the parable before us. The widow takes her petition to an earthly judge and keeps persisting until she gets true justice, even from an unjust judge. Now, our Lord Jesus was making a point here!

See Luke 18:6:

> *v6 And the Lord said, Hear what the unjust judge saith.*

Hear carefully! Listen and understand is what our Lord was declaring. He that has ears let him hear! This hearing isn't something that just passes through our ears. It is meditating, partaking of that Word!

I believe our Lord Jesus was saying with love and passion, "*Oh, my beloved ones, my precious sheep, hear now and understand what the unjust judge said in granting this widow her petition! Hear with open ears and open hearts! For your Heavenly Father, the Creator of all things, will answer you when you cry out to Him!*"

Do we not hear Him pleading with His beloved sheep to understand. He didn't just give them a good story. Jesus was giving The Truth about how God would respond to our cries! See the next two verses for confirmation.

Luke 18:7-8 declares:

> *v7 And shall not God avenge his own elect, which cry day and night unto him, though he bear long with them?*

v8 I tell you that he will avenge them speedily. Nevertheless when the Son of man cometh, shall he find faith on the earth?

It is very plain! Jesus tells us that our God will *"avenge His own elect."* The God and Father of our Lord Jesus Christ will carry out justice on our behalf. He will punish our adversary. He will vindicate us when we are accused.

There is an urgency present in the parable we are studying to bring our petitions to Father God. Not only this, but that we may know and understand that He will surely answer our petitions because God is Faithful and True. His Word came forth, making the decree that He would. Our Heavenly Father will not alter that which He proclaimed through the lips of His Holy Child Jesus Christ, our Lord! God will surely do what He said! (see Isaiah 55:11)

Consider now the last part of verse 7, *"though He bear long with them."* What does this mean? Jesus reveals the patient kindness of our Father. He bears with us when we lose heart, when we are discouraged, weary, faint, or just tired and want to give up. God is long-suffering towards us! This is what Jesus is revealing. The Father hears your cry, day and night, and He will avenge you of your adversary, speedily!

What does speedily mean in verse 8? After all, Jesus said God would judge for us speedily! See the *Strong's* definition below:

NT:5034 tachos (takh'-os); from the same as NT:5036; a brief space (of time), i.e. (with NT:1722 prefixed) in haste:

KJV - quickly, shortly, speedily.

It means; *"a brief space of time, in haste."* Our God will do it quickly. Yes, in His time! Remember, He bears long with our fainting. We may be fighting a great battle, which seems too difficult for us. But, God will surely deliver! We *"overcome by the Blood of The Lamb and the Word of our testimony"* (Revelation 12:11).

David said the following in 2 Samuel 22:30:

> *v30 For by thee I have run through a troop: by my God have I leaped over a wall.*

Through our God, we shall do the same! It may not look like it, we may not feel like we can, but through our God we shall. Thus the need for earnest prayer! This is a persistent prayer, which shows us the *"Power of Prayer"*!

Take note as well that Jesus addresses what fainting looks like. And, though our God bears long with us in our moments of weakness, He will answer the cry of our heart!

Look at the last part of Luke 18:8:

> *v8 Nevertheless when the Son of man cometh, shall he find faith on the earth?*

This is written as a loving rebuke, an admonition, for us to persist with faith in prayer.

Consider the following Scripture found in Jude 20-21:

> *v20 But ye, beloved, building up yourselves on your most holy faith, praying in the Holy Ghost,*

> *v21 Keep yourselves in the love of God, looking for the mercy of our Lord Jesus Christ unto eternal life.*

Jude, writing to the Church, tells us that we need to build ourselves up on *"most holy faith, Praying in the Holy Ghost."* The sentence structure reveals to us that faith in God is necessary for our fellowship with Him and that praying in the Holy Ghost builds us up in Him!

Jude writes in verse 3 that we should *"earnestly contend for the faith which was once delivered to the saints."* Faith produces an outward expression of the love we have for our God and for His beloved ones! Paul tells us that faith which works by love avails. *"For in Jesus Christ neither circumcision availeth anything, nor uncircumcision; but faith which worketh by love"* (Galatians 5:6). This is the faith we contend for, that we might love as our Lord Jesus, that we might be His instruments, though we think we have little, if anything, to offer. We press in until we obtain it!

Mark how there is power in this type of prayer. It takes us back to the real *"Purpose of Prayer."* We are asking our Heavenly Father for His Kingdom to come and His will to be done on the earth as it is in heaven. Not our will, Lord God, but yours be done!

Now, we know His will is that we have life and that more abundantly (John 10:10). We know that His will is that not one perish (John 3:16)! So, with this understanding, we press in to the heart of our Heavenly Father, asking for and seeking His Counsel, knocking until we obtain the thing He promised to give.

This doesn't mean we pray generally about something. It means that we seek the will of our Father about it. Then, we persist in prayer before Him, for His Word to be made manifest in the earth and in these earthen vessels.

Jesus came that He might destroy the works of the Devil (1 John 3:8). What are his works? He comes to steal, kill, and destroy. Jesus came that we might have abundant life, victory over the Enemy of our souls!

It is important to understand that we are to put our Lord in remembrance of His Word. He says we ought to remind Him. So, it must be important! See the following verse in Isaiah 43:26:

> *v26 Put me in remembrance: let us plead together: declare thou, that thou mayest be justified.*

We remind God of His Word concerning us, not any other word! We don't come to our Heavenly Father telling Him we are good for nothing pieces of garbage. We enter our Father's presence reminding Him of His great compassion and His promise to redeem us, not only ourselves personally, but all those He has given us love for. If we consider the previous verse in Isaiah, we understand what the Almighty wanted us to remind Him of.

Examine this verse in Isaiah 43:25:

v25 I, even I, am he that blotteth out thy transgressions for mine own sake, and will not remember thy sins.

It gives us something to shout about! The Holy One of Israel, our Blessed God, and Father of our Lord Jesus Christ tells us that He blots out our transgressions...all of them. He also tells us that He will not remember our sins! Bless His Holy Name! I am redeemed by the blood of Jesus Christ, my Lord. Our Heavenly Father declares He has blotted out my transgressions and will not remember my sins! He removed my sins from me as far as the east is from the west (Psalm 103:12). That means forever! After this, He tells us to remind Him of what He did! Listen, God already knows what He did, and He doesn't forget. Yet, He wants us to remember His Words and bring them to remembrance before Him. This is for our benefit! God wants to bless, but we need to bring ourselves, through faith, into the place of blessing. And, this is accomplished through the prayer of faith! God will answer even as He said because He is faithful! The Word of the Lord is forever settled in the heavens (Psalm 119:89). He cannot lie! This is the *"Power of Prayer"*! We have power with God through Jesus Christ, The Living Word. For, the very Words of our Lord confirm that God, our Father, wants to fellowship with us eternally. He, Himself, providing the means for fellowship to be restored. Ought it not follow then, since our Father loves us so much, that if we are in need of anything, He will provide it? He gave us His Holy Son. How shall He not? Contemplate the following passage of Scripture and see if this is not the case.

Romans 8:32 proclaims:

v32 He that spared not his own Son, but delivered him up for us all, how shall he not with him also freely give us all things?

The Love of God sustains us forever. If anything is lacking, He will see to it that we receive a full measure provided for us. We may be facing a trial that seems insurmountable but, nothing is impossible with our God. He is The Creator, and if something needs to be created to deliver us, He will do it. Jesus tells us that His judgment will be made on our behalf! We just need to persist through prayer to obtain what He tells us is already ours.

Here is another passage of Scripture that affirms the necessity of standing firm in prayer. Jesus, speaking to Peter, says in Mark 11:24:

> *v24 Therefore I say unto you, what things soever ye desire, when you pray, believe that ye receive them, and ye shall have them.*

Peter saw the fig tree that Jesus cursed was withered away (Mark 11:12-14, 20-21). The moment Jesus spoke to this tree, it ceased to live. They passed by that tree the very next morning, and Peter noticed it was dried up from the root, and he said something to Jesus about it. This isn't the common way a tree dies, which means what Jesus declared took place at the very root of the tree. Our Lord used this as a point of teaching and related it to prayer. So, speaking out is a form of prayer. In this case, it is making earnest supplication to God. Let's look at the Greek word used:

> *NT:4336 proseuchomai (pros-yoo'-khom-ahee); from NT:4314 and NT:2172; to pray to God, i.e., supplicate, worship:*
>
> *KJV - pray (X earnestly, for), make prayer.*

This word is used for prayer, supplication, and worship. Again, it reveals to us communion with our Heavenly Father. This doesn't mean we go around cursing fig trees. However, what can be understood from this is that there is power in what we say through faith.

Taking a closer look at the verses preceding this one, it becomes evident our faith in God is the key to powerful prayer because Jesus begins His teaching with, *"Have faith in God"* (Mark 11:22).

Jesus continues His instruction in verse 23. Pause and examine this for a moment! Look carefully at what our Lord Jesus speaks in Mark 11:23:

> *v23 For verily I say unto you, That whosoever shall say unto this mountain, Be thou removed, and be thou cast into the sea; and shall not doubt in his heart, but shall believe that those things which he saith shall come to pass; he shall have whatsoever he saith.*

Notice, Jesus didn't say you had to be someone special to walk in this anointing. All you need to be is you before God! Prayer is communion with Father God through Jesus Christ. So, there are no exclusions written here. Remember too, the words that our Lord Jesus speaks are Spirit and Life! He reveals to us here, as He teaches His disciples, God doesn't have respect of persons. He does not prefer you over me or vice versa! Our Heavenly Father just wants us to come in faith to Him, believing He will answer.

The struggle everyone faces at times is that we know and believe God can, but we aren't certain He will, for one reason or another. Maybe we feel unworthy, or it could be we think the thing we would like is too grand for us. Some of us might believe that what we are asking for is an insignificant thing and think maybe we shouldn't ask for it. Whatever reason we might have isn't really a valid one for failing to ask. Could it be that we really don't have faith enough to ask? This may be the real reason if we are honest with one another.

Jesus confronts these issues as He continues to teach His beloved disciples. He dispels the notion that you must be a prominent person or super holy! Jesus just uses the word *"whosoever"*! He spoke these words before! Where? John 3:15-16:

"Whosoever believeth in Him (Jesus) should not perish, but have eternal life." We received salvation by faith in Jesus Christ alone. Why not receive what He is speaking here too?

Our Lord continues by saying if you ask, not doubting, you shall have what you speak, declare. So, what does *"not doubting"* mean? Let's investigate the word used to find out. See the Greek word below:

> *NT:1252 diakrino (dee-ak-ree'-no); from NT:1223 and NT:2919; to separate thoroughly, i.e. (literally and reflexively) to withdraw from, or (by implication) oppose; figuratively, to discriminate (by implication, decide), or (reflexively) hesitate:*
>
> *KJV - contend, make (to) differ (-ence), discern, doubt, judge, be partial, stagger, waver.*

Observe its meanings! The word is a compound word from *dia* and *krino*. *Dia* is the channel of an act or through. *Krino* means to distinguish, try, or decide (mentally, or judicially); to try, condemn, or punish. Jesus was saying we are not to pass our own judgment about the thing we are asking for. Rather, let our hearts declare the matter as God calls it. In essence, our prayers must hold fast to what God has decreed concerning our situation. Jesus plainly says we can have what we are praying for if we don't wrongly decide about it.

Again, Jesus wasn't saying to go out and curse a fig tree to see if this works. Why? Because if you are trying to see if it works, you're already on the wrong footing. *Trying isn't moving in faith; it is moving in reason.* Faith is first toward God, believing He is who He said He is! It also stands that trusting God will give us what we've asked of Him, for one important reason, He said He would and He's a Good Father! Faith in God can move mountains. We just have to deal with unbelief in the heart, which are our thoughts and feelings, since Jesus says this is where unbelief resides. The thoughts and feelings we have about ourselves or others need to be brought to the cross and buried there. The reason others are included here is that Jesus continues with this same thought moving into verse 25, where He instructs us to be merciful and forgive. What does the Psalmist say? *"If I regard iniquity in my heart, The Lord will not hear me:"* (Psalm 66:18). So, if we refuse to forgive, we cannot expect God to respond to our prayer.

It is extremely important we understand that God wants to bless His beloved children. If we have come to Christ, we are His, and He will hear and answer our prayers.

I will offer one more Scripture before moving on to the next chapter just so we can see how much it pleases our Lord to answer our petitions. It is found in John 16:24:

> *v24 Hitherto have ye asked nothing in my name: ask, and ye shall receive, that your joy may be full.*

What a joy to know this is the heart of Father God and our beloved Saviour! He wants to grant us our petitions as we continue abiding in Him. Here is fellowship divine! This means we need to address our careless thoughts of our Heavenly Father towards us. May we grow in love and grace, believing what God says about us. Our thoughts about ourselves will affect our prayer life. But, God reveals to us His desire to answer, though at times He might decide on the best season to give us our request, and it may or may not fit with our schedule. The *"Power of Prayer"* is even more marvelous when we realize just how much more our fellowship grows as we commune with God, our Father, and our Lord Jesus Christ!

Consider other places in Scripture that demonstrate the *"Power of Prayer."* They are found in the Old Testament as well as the New Testament. We have many examples throughout the Bible that reveal this truth to us. Continue seeking, and you will be strengthened by every one of them.

Now we will turn our attention to the *"Position or Posture of Prayer"* we take before our Heavenly Father.

CHAPTER 3
The Position or Posture of Prayer

We've examined the *"Power of Prayer"* in Chapter Two, which is demonstrated through the prayer of faith. We also took note of Paul's letter to the Galatians. He revealed to us that circumcision doesn't avail in Christ, neither does uncircumcision. We found it is faith that works by love that avails with God. See the following verse in Galatians 5:6:

> *v6 For in Jesus Christ neither circumcision availeth anything, nor uncircumcision; but faith which worketh by love.*

Now let's turn our attention to the *"Position or Posture of Prayer."*

Thank you, Lord, our God, for revealing to us your Truth. Thank you for your unfailing love, Heavenly Father. Grant now that we may understand with hearing ears and hearts what you are declaring to us through our study in the Holy Name of Jesus Christ, our Lord! Guide us Holy Spirit into the very presence of our Heavenly Father and our Lord Jesus. Amen!

To begin, we understand by the Living Word of God that our Heavenly Father proved His eternal love for us through the perfect gift of His Son, our Lord Jesus Christ. This is the ultimate demonstration of love, the highest degree. Father God could give no greater gift! This being the truth, we begin to see the *"Position*

or Posture of Prayer" is always through love. Prayer, communion with God The Father and Jesus Christ His Son, begins, has its foundation in love. Every effectual fervent prayer has its origin in love, *"agape"*! True communion, fellowship with God The Father, God The Son, and God The Holy Ghost is always through this love!

Consider the following verse a moment in 1 Corinthians 13:13:

> *v13 And now abideth faith, hope, charity, these three; but the greatest of these is charity.*

There are three things listed here that abide in the heart of every child of God. The greatest is *"charity,"* love! This is *"agape"* love, not something inferior. This is the noblest of all loves, love in its highest form, as demonstrated by our Heavenly Father through the Gift of His Blessed Son Jesus Christ!

Note, *"charity,"* agape love, is the greatest of the three. If you will, love is the foundation stone upon which the others rest. Faith may be present, but without the foundation stone of love, it will not be enduring faith. Hope cannot rest alone, either. If one has hope, it must be grounded, settled, established in something steadfast. If not, hope is ill-founded! It must rest in truth, the truth that God is love, and He proved Himself to be so by the ultimate gift of love He offered to us.

Prayer rests upon the foundation of love! Why would a person want to fellowship with someone who doesn't truly love them? You may be acquainted with someone like this, but nothing meaningful or sustaining would ever come of it because mistrust would be present. So, you could never be yourself with a person such as this. There would always be a nagging thought or doubt about what the other person is thinking. Approaching our God from this perspective will never be fruitful. True fellowship rests in the knowledge that I am Loved, and my love is safe in this place!

The *"Position or Posture of Prayer"* is also with boldness and

humility, because of the great love that God has given to us. We come boldly, not in arrogance, but in confidence to God, because we know assuredly that He loves us, and He loves to commune with us! God doesn't look upon us as a second rate child. He doesn't view anyone with suspicion! He sees you and me through His blessed Son and considers us even as Christ because we are part of the *"Body of Christ."* Do we truly understand this?

How many lies have we believed regarding our position in Christ Jesus, our Lord? Listen, we may have stumbled, but we are not defeated. Let us rise to meet our Lord Jesus and glorify Him for the victory we have received in His blood and through His Holy Word! Hear His Words and no longer receive the lies of the enemy of our Lord Jesus. Stand now and see His salvation! His delights are with the sons of men, that means you and me. His love should then compel us, as it did Paul, to tell His story! Look what God has done for you and for me. Praise His Holy Name!

Consider our Lord Jesus and how He prayed earnestly to The Father. His posture in fellowship was always in love. He demonstrated His love for Father God in everything He did! Throughout the Gospels, we see Jesus often in prayer. He was seeking to establish the Kingdom of Father God and His will on the earth, even as it is in heaven. Jesus did this through communion with The Father in prayer. Yes, His Posture in fellowship was always in love. And, His Position, as He communed with God, was as a Son beloved of His Father. The following passages of Scripture confirm this John 17:24-26:

> *v24 Father, I will that they also, whom thou hast given me, be with me where I am; that they may behold my glory, which thou hast given me: for thou lovedst me before the foundation of the world.*
>
> *v25 O righteous Father, the world hath not known thee: but I have known thee, and these have known that thou hast sent me.*

v26 And I have declared unto them thy name, and will declare it: that the love wherewith thou hast loved me may be in them, and I in them.

This is how you and I can approach our Heavenly Father, as those who are in Christ Jesus! He is the Head of the Church, and we are His Bride! Father God looks at us and sees His Son. Hallelujah!!!

The *"Position or Posture of Prayer"* that our Lord Jesus lived out gives us an understanding of how we should come to our Father in Heaven! It also reveals to us that Father God will answer our petitions just as He did our Lord's. I realize in my case that I was once in bondage to doubts and fears, but no longer. I repent! Our Father in Heaven and our Blessed Lord Jesus are worthy of being trusted. The love God has for us has been demonstrated! It was manifest for all the world to see. Ought we not trust our God to do what He has promised? Do we trust Him in the fires and through the trials of this life to bring us through victoriously? Or, are we just barely going to make it? Lord, forgive us for doubting you and living by what we thought of you instead of getting to know your heart of love!

We recall that the *"Purpose of Prayer"* is to establish the Kingdom of God and His will in the earth. Jesus, through the *"Position or Posture of Prayer,"* confirms this and demonstrates the *"Power of Prayer."* As our Lord Jesus was in fellowship through prayer, He listened for Father God's counsel. He then walked in obedience to God's instruction that He might glorify His Father. Jesus often went out to pray. It wasn't a one-time thing. Jesus was in constant communion with God. There were moments when His prayers were heard by those around Him, such as when Lazarus was raised from the dead. Then, there were times when Jesus went out to be alone with His Father being in prayer all night. One such time was when He set some of the disciples apart, calling them Apostles. See the verses referenced in Luke 6:12-13:

v12 And it came to pass in those days, that he went out into a mountain to pray, and continued all night in prayer to God.

v13 And when it was day, he called unto him his disciples: and of them he chose twelve, whom also he named apostles;

He was always in communion with Father God, seeking only to do His will. This is evidenced throughout His entire life. What are we able to glean from this? We, too, can walk in constant fellowship with Father God and our Lord Jesus Christ, praying in The Holy Ghost for *"His Kingdom to come and His will to be done in the earth as it is in heaven."* We pray with the knowledge that our Father in Heaven, who is not a respecter of persons, will respond to our petitions even as He did our Lord Jesus. Why? Because our Lord declared this to be so! Jesus didn't lie! Our God will hear and answer our cries even as we have come to understand through our study of Luke 18:1-8.

Again, Jesus finished the parable of the unjust judge with the following question. *"Nevertheless when the Son of man cometh, shall he find faith on the earth?"* How will you and I answer that question? For, it is certain, we will!

The *"Position or Posture of Prayer"* is through faith, which works by love. This being the case, we must know and understand that this faith is in and through our God! Why? Because God is Love! And, this faith has its origin in The Almighty God Himself! Jesus Christ is the Author of our Faith, and He is the Finisher of our Faith as well. He will complete this work of faith in us, by, in, through love! For, this love is of God who spoke all things into being from His very heart of love!

Consider this; creation was born of love! It wasn't something that just happened. It wasn't brought forth by some form of cosmic energy! Creation was brought forth by love. Creation, before the fall of man, demonstrated the glory of the God of love. Everything moved in a rhythm of love. It was a rebellion against the Almighty God that brought about the chaos that is now present in this world. However, God, through His Holy Child, Jesus Christ, has decreed that this chaos will soon come to an end. He will establish His Kingdom of Righteousness, Peace, and Joy in the Holy Ghost upon the earth even as it is in heaven above. Our earnest prayers in the Spirit agree with Father God for this transformation to take place. And, it is written: *"Ask, and it shall be given."* So, let us ask in faith, knowing that our God will surely answer our petitions!

It is the Love of God that brings us out of darkness into His Marvelous Light! So, it is necessary to understand that coming out of darkness is a war. Take, for example, the children of Israel as they were delivered out of the hand of Pharaoh. Consider how deliverance came about. They cried unto the Lord, and He heard their cry! The children of Israel prayed for deliverance, and God sent a Deliverer! They were treated harshly by Pharaoh during this deliverance, but the Egyptians gave them of their substance as God decreed! They were pursued by the ones who afflicted them even after they were sent away with the bounty of their captors! God overthrew the Egyptians as they pursued them through the sea! Then the children of Israel found they would have to fight giants, and fear came upon them! They had to wander in the desert because of their unbelief! Their children were brought into the Promised Land by faith! The seed of Abraham possessed the land, were removed from the land, brought back to the land, and still, the promise of God is being manifest upon His people. The final day is coming!

All of these things reveal to us the love and mercy of God. It also bears witness to the trials of faith! The outcome is not always what we think it should be. However, when we hear His promise, He will finish what He started, we can shout knowing the victory is ours through Jesus Christ our Lord! We will have desert experiences and trials because they are part of life. The enemy of our souls hates us, but God will bring us out as He promised. As we understand this, we say as David did in Psalm 108:13: *"through God we shall do valiantly."* David testifies of the mercy of the Almighty God who delivers us though we have faltered and been faithless many times. He turned his prayer back to God, knowing the great mercies of God endure forever, and His faithfulness is beyond measure. Likewise, through His Holy love and mercy, He comes to set us free.

David touches the heart of Father God through his posture in prayer. As a son before his blessed Father, David beseeches Him to deliver. Then proclaims that God will give him the strength to do valiantly because he confidently rests in the love that The Father has for him! He declares God's Word of truth and love back to Him.

Jesus says in Luke 12:32:

> *v32 Fear not, little flock; for it is your Father's good pleasure to give you the kingdom.*

He also said in Luke 18:16-17:

> *v16 But Jesus called them unto him, and said, Suffer little children to come unto me, and forbid them not: for of such is the kingdom of God.*
>
> *v17 Verily I say unto you, Whosoever shall not receive the kingdom of God as a little child shall in no wise enter therein.*

It is important to recognize that we must come to God as a little child. This reveals son-ship. Our *"Position or Posture of Prayer"* is as a child of God. Father God views us this way with delight. He declares to us through the very Words of our Lord Jesus that His good pleasure is to give us the Kingdom! So, if His delight is to give us the Kingdom, why would He withhold any portion from us that relates to His Kingdom?

Paul, writing to the Romans, gives us a picture of the Kingdom of God Romans 14:17:

v17 For the kingdom of God is not meat and drink; but righteousness, and peace, and joy in the Holy Ghost.

This is right standing as a child of God with our Heavenly Father, with all the privileges of a child. We have access to the throne room of grace through the blood of Jesus Christ! Petitions are gladly heard and granted from the throne of grace. Wisdom is freely offered there too. Power is given from this wonderful place as well, equipping us to walk in this righteousness by the Holy Ghost.

Our Father in Heaven doesn't limit His free grace to us. We may not be like Peter, John, Paul, or any of the other Apostles, and frankly, we weren't called to be like them. We were called to be who we are in Christ Jesus our Lord, united with Him in love and power, walking out the life He gave us to walk as new creations in Christ!

The Kingdom of God also provides for our peace! We have peace with God through the blood of our Lord Jesus! This is heart peace! We also have soul peace freely given to us, which governs our thoughts about who we are before our Heavenly Father. We aren't orphans any longer! We are sons and daughters of the Most High God with all that pertains to being children given to us by God through the power of The Holy Ghost, who imparts the very peace of God within us.

Bless The Lord; we also receive joy through the Holy Spirit in our lives. He affirms us as children of The Most High God, He instructs us in the ways of our Father, and delights in revealing to us the hidden things of God.

All these things pertain to the Kingdom of God, which our Heavenly Father delights in bestowing upon us! So, our *"Position or Posture of Prayer"* is as His beloved children as well. We are invited to relate to our Heavenly Father just as our Lord Jesus did! We have that privilege, though we don't exercise it as often as we ought!

The enemy of our souls may be pursuing just as David's enemy pursued him. But, God will judge our enemy and vindicate us speedily! He has spoken, and He will surely do it! Some may experience hardships for a season, even as the Israelites did under Pharaoh. However, God will bring us out! We don't know how our God will do it. We don't know how many battles we will face before we reach the Promised Land of heaven. Nevertheless, God, our Father, who demonstrated His Love through Jesus Christ, His Son will surely bring us safely home to Himself. For, heaven is our Promised Land, and we will abide with Him forever! Praise His Holy Name!!! Let us continue to recall and rehearse what we have studied as we move forward now to our *"Place of Prayer."*

CHAPTER 4
The Place of Prayer

We should recap some things before exploring the *"Place of Prayer."* First, we see that the *"Purpose of Prayer"* is to establish the Kingdom of God and His will in the earth through our communion with Him. Second, the *"Power of Prayer,"* as we walk in communion with Father God and our Lord Jesus, is through faith, which works by love, having its very foundation and origin in God Himself. Third, we understand that the *"Position or Posture of Prayer"* is always in this love, with a childlike heart, knowing we are His beloved children! Further, it was revealed to us how much God wants to answer the prayers of His precious children.

Now, by the grace of our Lord, we will contemplate the *"Place of Prayer."*

Father God, we come now to you in the Holy Name of Jesus Christ our Lord seeking your counsel regarding the *"Place of Prayer."* Holy Spirit, reveal this to our hearts. We lay aside our suppositions since we do not yet know as we ought. Lead us onward, I pray, into the truth even as our Lord Jesus said you would. This we ask, Father God, according to your will, and we thank you for it in Jesus' Lovely Name! Amen.

Remembering that the *"Position or Posture of Prayer"* is always in and through love, we come to the *"Place of Prayer."* The *"Place of Prayer"* begins with love, the love of God our Father, and Jesus

Christ, our Lord, His Holy Son! This is demonstrated at the Cross of Jesus Christ, where all the sins and iniquities written against us were nailed!

Consider these verses in Colossians 2:13-15:

v13 And you, being dead in your sins and the uncircumcision of your flesh, hath he quickened together with him, having forgiven you all trespasses;

v14 Blotting out the handwriting of ordinances that was against us, which was contrary to us, and took it out of the way, nailing it to his cross;

v15 And having spoiled principalities and powers, he made a shew of them openly, triumphing over them in it.

And in Colossians 1:19-22:

v19 For it pleased the Father that in him should all fulness dwell;

v20 And, having made peace through the blood of his cross, by him to reconcile all things unto himself; by him, I say, whether they be things in earth, or things in heaven.

v21 And you, that were sometime alienated and enemies in your mind by wicked works, yet now hath he reconciled

v22 In the body of his flesh through death, to present you holy and unblameable and unreproveable in his sight:

The *"Place of Prayer,"* in love, begins at the Cross of Jesus Christ, our Lord. For there, the weight and guilt of sin were forever destroyed. Through the Cross of our Lord Jesus Christ, we have been quickened together with Him! Hallelujah! I behold the wondrous work of Jesus, my Lord, there at the cross, and through the blood that Jesus shed, I am set free forevermore! He took away everything that was written against me and you. Everything! Chapter 2 Verse 13 gives us great cause to rejoice that it was even while we were in our sins Jesus did this marvelous work for us. It says: *"And you, being dead in your sins..."* This implies a present condition. The words *"being dead"* meaning at that very moment. Bless the Name of our Lord Jesus. He did this work for us while we were still enemies of God, according to His great mercies! So then, the *"Place of Prayer"* begins at the cross, which demonstrates the love of God for us! Now, through the blood of the everlasting Covenant, we have access to the throne room of grace. In the cross and through the cross of Jesus, we have the liberty to stand in the presence of our Heavenly Father. This is because of His marvelous love. He loves us so much that He gave His only begotten Son for our ransom. So complete is this work that the blood of Jesus Christ fulfilled the whole of God's requirement for our justification before Him.

It is through the precious blood of Christ Jesus we overcome according to Revelation 12:11, which says:

> *v11 And they overcame him by the blood of the Lamb, and by the word of their testimony; and they loved not their lives unto the death.*

We recognize our right standing with God as we stand in this *"Place of Prayer."* We then confess the truth of God's Word, which has become our testimony in this *"Place of Prayer."* We are under the Everlasting Covenant of the blood of Jesus Christ, the Lamb of God. And, we are under the Covenant Promise of His Everlasting Word!

The *"Place of Prayer"* grants us liberty and access to our Heavenly Father. We contemplated the following verse previously, but let's review it again.

Romans 8:32 reads:

> *v32 He that spared not his own Son, but delivered him up for us all, how shall he not with him also freely give us all things?*

See what is granted to us by the gracious Gift of our Heavenly Father? We place our complete trust in the One who was made a surety for us through His death upon the Cross. All this He did with Love for us, and as we receive Him and His offering, we are given the blessed hope of Life Eternal according to the promise of God our Father.

John declared it to us in this fashion in 1 John 5:10-11:

> *v10 He that believeth on the Son of God hath the witness in himself: he that believeth not God hath made him a liar; because he believeth not the record that God gave of his Son.*

> *v11 And this is the record, that God hath given to us eternal life, and this life is in his Son.*

God has given us Eternal Life, and this Life is in His Son! From this *"Place of Prayer,"* we can come boldly before our Father in heaven. And, according to His Word, He will grant our petitions as we humble ourselves before Him!

Let us consider our ways before Him, humbling ourselves in prayer, and seek His Face. For surely, as it is written, He will hear our petitions as we turn from our own wicked ways, and He will heal our land.

2 Chronicles 7:14 reads:

> *v14 If my people, which are called by my name, shall humble themselves, and pray, and seek my face, and turn from their wicked ways; then will I hear from heaven, and will forgive their sin, and will heal their land.*

The pride and arrogance of man will always seek a way around the Cross. Why? Paul tells us that it is because to those who are perishing, it is foolishness. 1 Corinthians 1:18:

> *v18 For the preaching of the cross is to them that perish*

foolishness; but unto us which are saved it is the power of God.

Again we read in 1 Corinthians 1:23-24:

v23 But we preach Christ crucified, unto the Jews a stumblingblock, and unto the Greeks foolishness;

v24 But unto them which are called, both Jews and Greeks, Christ the power of God, and the wisdom of God.

Paul confirms to us the significance of the preaching of the Cross, which is where we see the *"Place of Prayer"* begin. It is the *"Power of God."* The message of Christ crucified is *"Christ the Power of God, and the Wisdom of God"* to deliver all who are bound in sin!

Just as love is the foundation stone for faith and hope, so the *"Place of Prayer"* begins with the demonstration of God's great love for us, revealing to us the Glory of God! It is as the old song declares: *"At the Cross, at the Cross, where I first saw the Light, and the burden of my heart rolled away. It was there by faith I received my sight, and now I am happy all the day.[2]"*

This is where faith towards God had its beginning. And, in the Cross is where our faith will find its ending, where faith will become sight! Praise God for His marvelous love to us!

From this *"Place of Prayer,"* our heartfelt petition before our Father is for the fullness of His Kingdom to come *"as it is in heaven, so on earth."* This is our desire as sons and daughters of the Most High God. For, we are now a new creation in Christ Jesus, our Lord; old desires are passed away! We also seek to renew our minds as Paul the Apostle taught. How is this accomplished? It is done by seeking and listening for the voice of our Lord Jesus throughout His Word and dwelling, abiding, in His Words!

---

[2] Song, *At the Cross*, written by Isaac Watts, published in 1707

Paul wrote in Philippians 4:8-9:

> *v8 Finally, brethren, whatsoever things are true, whatsoever things are honest, whatsoever things are just, whatsoever things are pure, whatsoever things are lovely, whatsoever things are of good report; if there be any virtue, and if there be any praise, think on these things.*

> *v9 Those things, which ye have both learned, and received, and heard, and seen in me, do: and the God of peace shall be with you.*

Paul instructed us to meditate upon things which come of the truth, by the truth, and through the truth! The Apostle Paul is not talking of something we *think* is the truth, but that which *is* the Truth. There is only one truth, which upholds all things, and this is the Living Word of God. Paul gives these guidelines for renewing our minds, and in verse 9 tells us as we walk in them, doing them, the *"God of peace shall be with you."* Praise the Lord! This is what we desire as sons and daughters of God. The promise of His Holy Peace is guaranteed as we abide in Christ, renewing our minds in Him. I did not say that trials wouldn't come. Rather, Jesus Christ, our Lord, will never leave us no matter what we face!

Paul also wrote the following in his letter to the Philippians. Philippians 2:5-8:

> *v5 Let this mind be in you, which was also in Christ Jesus:*

> *v6 Who, being in the form of God, thought it not robbery to be equal with God:*

> *v7 But made himself of no reputation, and took upon him the form of a servant, and was made in the likeness of men:*

> *v8 And being found in fashion as a man, he humbled himself, and became obedient unto death, even the death of the cross.*

We are to have the same mind as our Lord Jesus. From the *"Place of Prayer,"* in truth, we yield ourselves that we may be like our Lord Jesus. He didn't think it was robbery or strange that He was equal with Father God. He didn't boast of those things though He had every right to do so! Rather, Jesus humbled Himself before God, *"humbled Himself, and became obedient unto death, even the death of the cross."* This is the Cross through which we have been given Eternal Life! The heart of our Lord Jesus was to obey God, The Father! He became obedience!

What does obedience mean? In Greek, it is the word *"hupakouo."* According to *Strong's Concordance,* it is defined as:

> *NT 5219 hupakouo (hoop-ak-oo'-o); from NT:5259 and NT:191; to hear under (as a subordinate), i.e., to listen attentively; by implication, to heed or conform to a command or authority:*
>
> *KJV - hearken, be obedient to, obey.*

It means to listen attentively and to heed or conform to a command or authority. Jesus didn't just hear what Father God said. He conformed Himself to God's will. He made Himself of no reputation. Jesus took upon Himself the will of God to rescue this lost and dying world from the bondage of sin, though it meant He was asked to yield His own Life in order that it might be accomplished.

So, we are instructed to have the same mind, which means we commit our lives to God, The Father, for the sake of His Kingdom and His Will, not our own, though we are standing in the righteousness of Jesus Christ as His sons and daughters. We have the privileges of heaven, and through these privileges, we speak what Jesus speaks. We listen for His precious Word and move in obedience to His command in order that Father God might be glorified in the earth, that souls may be birthed into the Kingdom of God, even as He wills!

In Christ Jesus, we have abundant life; though we are commanded to humble ourselves for the sake of our brothers, some of whom have not as yet been birthed into the Kingdom. This doesn't mean we live with a poor mentality, but with a pouring mentality! I live to shine forth the goodness of God so that others may live, and this life is through my death; death to my own will, my own ways, my own passions. I live, though I die, as Paul said in Galatians 2:20.

I have a life that is richer in love and graces! I am filled with hope and peace! I have been given *"everything that pertains to life and Godliness"* through the Cross of Jesus Christ! It is in Christ Jesus, our Lord, that we have the *"Abundant Life."* Apart from Him, there is no real life and certainly no lasting fruit! The preaching of the Cross is to the world foolishness, as it is written. However, to those who are saved, *"it is the power of God."*

This is the *"Place of Prayer"* in the Cross! I have a new life, right now, because of what my Lord Jesus accomplished through obedience to God, our Father, at the Cross! If our Lord had not obeyed Father God, we would not have life. Rather, we would have been judged unfit for the Kingdom of God! Bless His Holy Name, Jesus gave Himself for us so that we might live. Now, through Christ, we are reconciled to God and have the right, the power, to bring others to reconciliation!

There is something else we should reflect upon regarding the *"Place of Prayer."* It is found in Isaiah 56:7:

> *v7 Even them will I bring to my holy mountain, and make them joyful in my house of prayer: their burnt offerings and their sacrifices shall be accepted upon mine altar; for mine house shall be called an house of prayer for all people.*

Jesus referred to this passage of Scripture in Matthew 21:13. He cast out those who were buying and selling in the temple saying:

> *v21 It is written, My house shall be called the house of*

prayer; but ye have made it a den of thieves.

These verses are referring to the temple of God here on earth, the place where God chose to put His Name. As I was considering this in prayer, the Holy Spirit dropped 1 Corinthians 6:19-20 into my heart:

> *v19 What? know ye not that your body is the temple of the Holy Ghost which is in you, which ye have of God, and ye are not your own?*
>
> *v20 For ye are bought with a price: therefore glorify God in your body, and in your spirit, which are God's.*

It caused me to pause and reflect deeply as I rehearsed this in my heart. I heard the voice of my Lord saying, *"My temple is a house of prayer, and since I now reside in you, should you not also be a house of prayer?"* The more I meditated upon this, the more I could understand its depth. Jesus drove out those who were buying and selling in the temple; they had made the House of God a den of thieves. The Holy Spirit spoke to me and asked, *"If you don't make the Temple of your heart, a Place of Prayer, what are you selling?"* My heart is the dwelling place of my Saviour! It ought to be a consecrated place of prayer because Jesus is the Great High Priest. He is ever interceding for us, and since I was *"bought with a price,"* His precious blood, my heart should now become a temple He intercedes through! This is why Paul exclaims, *"therefore glorify God in your body, and in your spirit, which are God's."* We are commanded to walk in the Spirit, not after the flesh. Otherwise, what we offer is not the true Gospel. If we would walk in the Spirit before God, living our lives in submission to Jesus Christ, we would better reflect the image of our Saviour!

So then, our bodies being a temple where Christ dwells is also a *"Place of Prayer,"* where we seek the Face of God for His Kingdom and His will to be established. Our hearts are a place for His abiding presence and a place of intimate communion with our

Heavenly Father and our Lord Jesus Christ! Lord Jesus, we present ourselves to you that you might make it so! Amen!

Before we depart from the *"Place of Prayer,"* contemplate if you will, what is now ours through the Cross of Christ, and the dwelling place of His presence within us! Meditate much upon this!

Jesus is the door through which we enter into the green pastures He has prepared for us (John 10:9). So, enter and enjoy the goodness of His Love!

In the next chapter, we will give contemplation to the *"Pleading and Persistence of Prayer."*

CHAPTER 5
The Pleading & Persistence of Prayer

Our prayer, Holy Father, is that we might know you through this study. We cannot hope to comprehend if you don't open the eyes and ears of our understanding, to see and hear clearly. So, this is our prayer blessed Heavenly Father. Jesus told us that it is your good pleasure to give us the Kingdom. We ask for your Kingdom to come as we continue this study. I thank you, blessed Lord, for the promises of your Word. You said if we ask we will receive. Therefore, I praise you, Oh Lord Most High, for granting the desire of our hearts in the lovely Name of Jesus Christ. Amen!

Bless the Lord, we realize that we can come to Him with our petitions, and He will grant them. Because, we are not seeking for ourselves alone, but for the sake of our Father's will. We want the Body of Christ to be made whole, and we know there is no flaw in Christ Jesus, our Lord. Likewise, there is no flaw in His holy Body, of which we are a part. We aren't some discarded item! We are a working part of the Body of Jesus Christ, our Lord. He is the Head, and we are members of His holy Body! Not everyone is the same, thank God, or else the Body would be dysfunctional. Each person is uniquely equipped to shine forth the Glory of God by his or her uniqueness! Through this uniqueness in Jesus, we manifest the love (Glory) of God, revealing His beauty in earthen vessels.

Prayer is the avenue through which we commune with our Heavenly Father! He delights in our coming to Him and seeking

His Face! Thus far, we briefly examined the *"Purpose of Prayer,"* the *"Power of Prayer,"* the *"Position or Posture of Prayer,"* and the *"Place of Prayer."* I say only briefly because there is a great deal more we could explore regarding these insights into prayer. However, this study is meant to get us started and spur us to continue seeking.

Now we come to the *"Pleading and Persistence of Prayer."* There are many places in Scripture we could examine, which represent this pillar of prayer. However, I think it best to consider the prayers that our Lord Jesus offered to Father God. There are texts we could investigate that reveal to us how often our Lord prayed, which also gives insight into His faithful persistence with Father God. For instance, we know there are times He prayed all night, though we don't know what He asked The Father about. We could surmise some of these things given the ministry which followed. Still, it may be best to consider some of the prayers our Lord Jesus offered, which disclose His fervent desire to see The Father's will established in the earth.

Let us attentively ponder the *"Pleading and Persistence of Prayer."* We may study one segment of this and find another truth revealed to us as well. Moving forward, may our hearts observe closely what our Lord is saying by the Holy Spirit!

The passage of Scripture I would like to examine closely is found in John Chapter 17. This prayer is the signature prayer of our Lord Jesus. He reveals to us His whole heart as He pours out this prayer to The Father before His disciples. There are other prayers that our Lord offered to God that shine the Light of God's love forth. But, this prayer is the culmination of our Lord's work before the Cross. Read the whole of this chapter carefully, and you will see the love of our Lord manifest.

As we examine and reflect upon these things, it is important for us to remember that the *"Place of Prayer"* begins at the Cross. For, through the Cross of Jesus Christ, we were brought forth from darkness into His Glorious Light! We consider the *"Pleading and Persistence of Prayer"* from this place of redemption because, at the Cross, we have been born again, translated from the kingdom of darkness into the Kingdom of Light! Now, the prayer that Jesus prays should spur us to ask likewise.

Observe the first six verses of John 17 carefully.

It is written in John 17:1-6:

> *v1 These words spake Jesus, and lifted up his eyes to heaven, and said, Father, the hour is come; glorify thy Son, that thy Son also may glorify thee:*
>
> *v2 As thou hast given him power over all flesh, that he should give eternal life to as many as thou hast given him.*
>
> *v3 And this is life eternal, that they might know thee the only true God, and Jesus Christ, whom thou hast sent.*
>
> *v4 I have glorified thee on the earth: I have finished the work which thou gavest me to do.*
>
> *v5 And now, O Father, glorify thou me with thine own self with the glory which I had with thee before the world was.*
>
> *v6 I have manifested thy name unto the men which thou gavest me out of the world: thine they were, and thou gavest them me; and they have kept thy word.*

It is vital for us to clearly understand what our Lord Jesus was asking for since it reflects His heart towards Father God. To be certain, it was not a selfish prayer! This prayer was for The Father in heaven to be glorified in Him! Look at the last part of verse 1. Jesus asks The Father to, *"glorify thy Son that thy Son also may glorify Thee."* This is most undeniably a prayer for Father God to be exalted! Our Lord doesn't ask for glory for Himself alone. Jesus wants Father God to be glorified in Him, though it may be extremely difficult for Jesus Himself.

What is the *"Glory of God"*? The word in the Greek means to bring honor, glory, dignity, praise, and worship. I think it important we go further in thought here. This was translated into Greek, but Jesus was Hebrew. So, what does Glory mean in Hebrew? It means, only in a good sense, the abounding weight of glory, honor, and splendor! I personally believe that Jesus is referring to the very nature of God in fullness! I also believe that Jesus makes known what this glory looks like as this prayer continues.

This can be seen in verse 24 of this Chapter. Jesus says:

> *v24 Father, I will that they also, whom thou hast given me, be with me where I am; that they may behold my glory, which thou hast given me: for thou lovedst me before the foundation of the world.*

This is what Jesus is referring to as He is praying. He is revealing to us the glory of God, and this glory is His everlasting love! Jesus was asking The Father that all who are given to Him would be able to behold His glory, which God The Father had given Him even before the foundation of the world. And, the glory of God is expressed as The Father's everlasting Love! This is the glory that Jesus is praying for in verses 1 through 6. Can we see what is expressed through these precious words?

The surpassing love of God, the glory of Father God, is beyond description. It transcends the depths of our imagination! Another passage of Scripture that gives a glimpse of His all-surpassing glory is found in Revelation 21:23, which reads:

> *v23 And the city had no need of the sun, neither of the moon, to shine in it: for the glory of God did lighten it, and the lamb is the light thereof.*

The glory God has given to His Son is infinitely greater than any star of heaven! No sun, no star can compare to the glory of God as disclosed here. This is the manifest love of God for His Son expressed, which we will one day behold and partake of!

Jesus prays that God would glorify Him, manifest His everlasting love through Him, so that He might also pour out this same glory, love, back to The Father. His prayer was a holy offering back to God, reflecting all honor to Him.

Our Heavenly Father answered our Lord's prayer. As we observed in Revelation 21:23, one day, the veil over our eyes will be removed, and we will see the surpassing glory of God, the fullness of His love shining as the Eternal Light of creation.

We are commissioned to bring glory to our God, Father, Son, and Holy Ghost, as Jesus did. How is this done? It isn't through careless worship or living. It is through love, which only comes from Him! It is a reflection of Jesus. We glorify God through our love, which is in Christ. This is the first command and the last! Love the Lord your God with your whole being is the first command (Deuteronomy 6:5). The next is; love one another as our Lord Jesus commanded (Leviticus 9:18, Matthew 22:37, Mark 12:30, John 15:12)! This is what glorifies God, the thing that pleases Him most! There is no other sacrifice, apart from love, that has greater value. As a matter of fact, every offering we give to God must be from this position. Love is where God began with us, as demonstrated by the blessed gift of His Holy Son. It was by this same love that Jesus gave Himself as an offering for our sins. Likewise, it is in love through Christ Jesus that our gifts are acceptable. Without the love of God in our hearts, we are a *"sounding brass, or a tinkling cymbal,"* just noisemakers (1 Corinthians 13:1).

I say then that the pleading of our Lord Jesus is what we also begin with as we come through the Cross. We may not be there in degree yet. However, if we belong to Christ, this will be our plea. Father God, glorify your Name in me that I may bring you glory! In other words, love through me, Oh Lord, that your love may be manifest in the earth. Fill me with your love that others may come to know your glorious love!

Pleading implies fervency and tenacity! This is depicted as seen in Luke 22:44:

> v22 *And being in an agony he prayed more earnestly: and his sweat was as it were great drops of blood falling down to the ground.*

Jesus did not change His course of action because He saw trials ahead. He was in great agony! Yet, Jesus prayed more earnestly for strength to finish what was before Him. He knew what He would face and told His disciples of these things before they came to pass. However, Jesus didn't alter His ministry to keep Himself from the suffering that would come. He maintained the cause of Father God. He declared the will of God and was fervent in devotion to Him throughout His life.

Christ Jesus, our Lord, made His plea for God's glory to be seen before the Cross so that the love of our Heavenly Father might be demonstrated through Him upon the Cross and be confirmed as God raised Him from the dead. Jesus was assured that He would be with The Father soon. He wasn't just trying to make it through this horrific ordeal. He wanted the splendor of The Father's love to be clearly seen in Him and given to others through Him!

The prayer of Jesus in John 17 reveals not only the pleading with God but our Lord's persistence with God too. Jesus said that He came to do the will of The Father, and throughout the life of Christ, this was displayed. His prayer reveals to us clearly that it was our Lord's desire, even through the agony of the days before Him and through the death of the Cross, to glorify His Father in heaven. He wanted the love of Father God to be displayed even through His death! Our Lord Jesus lived upon this earth as a man. He felt what we feel, though He never sinned. He was rejected like no other! He was despised like no other! He experienced the beatings that were ours to bear. He wore a crown of thorns that mocked His love! He died upon the Cross to redeem us from our sins and was raised again for our justification. All this He did to glorify His Father and manifest The Father's love for us. This is *"Persistence in Prayer"* and a testimony of His love.

The Father heard the pleading of our Lord Jesus and rewarded His persistence! Jesus most wholly and completely revealed God's love through His example. Father God answered His prayer, and now Jesus is seated at His right hand, still interceding for the will of our Father in Heaven to be done in the earth.

Again, as we go through this prayer, we see the love of Jesus for Father God and for His sheep. He isn't praying for Himself but is wholly giving Himself to the will of God, our Father. It is not the will of God that any perish, and Jesus is seeking the will of God yet again for His beloved ones. See how this prayer confirms the love of God and the *"Pleading and Persistence of Prayer"*?

We have been given this same mandate, if you will. Jesus gave us the command to *"love one another,"* and the picture of love He was speaking of is manifest in His life and prayer here! The Apostles of our Lord walked in this love, as is witnessed in the Scriptures. This is what love looks like as we plead with God, our Father, for His Kingdom to come! The prayer of our hearts joins with our Lord that He might fulfill His Word in and through us. We may not be called to give our lives as some. However, we are called to lay down our lives for our brethren. This is dying to ourselves, our own wishes, for Christ's sake. As we do, we too will make known the everlasting love of God through our lives to others. Oh Father God, let the love of Christ Jesus, our Lord, be manifest in our hearts. Fill us with your glory and your precious holy love, in the Name of Jesus Christ, our Lord, we ask! Amen.

As I've said before, there are other places in Scripture that we could contemplate regarding the *"Pleading and Persistence of Prayer."* But, I believe this is the most beautiful example we could gaze upon. It is the glory of God displayed in the Face of Jesus Christ, our Lord, God's love expressed. No other thing can compare with this!

Let's rest here a while and behold the glory, the love of our God, and our Saviour Jesus Christ before continuing on to the *"Promises of Prayer."* Blessed be the Name of our Lord, who loves us with an everlasting love! I marvel and rejoice as I behold His love in this most gracious green pasture!

CHAPTER 6
The Promises of Prayer

Now we will reflect upon the *"Promises of Prayer."* As I've said before, there are many Scriptures we could examine, which would be of great value regarding the Promises of God through prayer. However, for this study, I believe we should consider one of the passages found in Mark Chapter 11. But, before we begin, let us seek through prayer for wisdom and instruction through our Great Comforter!

Holy God, our Father, we come in the Blessed Name of Jesus Christ and ask now for wisdom and instruction that you have promised us through the counsel of your precious Holy Spirit. We invite you here, blessed God! We praise and worship your Most Holy Name, and we welcome you as our Great Counselor and Teacher. Fill us now with your understanding as we seek to know you through your Holy Word! I thank you now for revealing yourself to us even as you have promised, and I bless your glorious Most Holy Name, Heavenly Father, through our Blessed Saviour Jesus Christ, our Lord, Amen, and Amen!

It seems to me that we have missed a great deal regarding the promises that Father God has given us through His precious Holy Word. Even if we can quote them chapter and verse, it appears that we have missed the heart of our Heavenly Father in the giving of these promises. I believe we should continue to seek the counsel of the Holy Spirit, so we don't miss the heart of the promises as we gaze upon them. As we study the verses in Mark, let us continue to focus upon the very heart of Father God in the Face of our Lord Jesus.

Let's look into the heart of our Heavenly Father now as we consider the following verses in Mark 11:21-26:

> *v21 And Peter calling to remembrance saith unto him, Master, behold the fig tree which thou cursedst is withered away.*
>
> *v22 And Jesus answering saith unto them, Have faith in God.*
>
> *v23 For verily I say unto you, That whosoever shall say unto this mountain, Be thou removed, and be thou cast into the sea; and shall not doubt in his heart, but shall believe that those things which he saith shall come to pass; he shall have whatsoever he saith.*
>
> *v24 Therefore I say unto you, What things soever ye desire, when ye pray, believe that ye receive them, and ye shall have them.*
>
> *v25 And when ye stand praying, forgive, if ye have ought against any: that your Father also which is in heaven may forgive you your trespasses.*
>
> *v26 But if ye do not forgive, neither will your Father which is in heaven forgive your trespasses.*

I believe it is important to consider the context and the One who is counseling here. Jesus Christ, our Blessed Saviour, is giving revelation into the simplistic, childlike way we are to approach our God when communing with Him through prayer; and how we are to make our declarations regarding His Kingdom being manifest. Some may not view this passage this way. However, I am often reminded that Jesus came to do the will of Father God, and this is how I believe we are to gaze upon this lesson our Lord Jesus taught.

So, what took place and what was the lesson our Lord was teaching in this example? There are other questions that could be submitted, though I think it best for now to consider these two.

Peter reminded Jesus that He cursed this fig tree and that it was now *"withered away."* The day before Jesus did curse the fig tree because He came to it expecting fruit, which apparently the tree should have been producing, but there was none. So, Jesus cursed the tree because it was unfruitful. Low and behold, the very next morning, while passing by this fig tree, they noticed it had dried up from the roots. Clearly, the words Jesus spoke over the tree brought about its demise. The fig tree died! It's as simple as that. Jesus cursed it, and it died! We could go to a number of places with this. But, I still think it is important to remember what Jesus said He came to do! He came to do the will of The Father, even in this! Yes, even through this example, Jesus wasn't self-seeking. He was Father-seeking!

Consider, our blessed Heavenly Father is the Great Husbandman! Jesus reveals this in John, Chapter 15. This plant wasn't doing what Father God had commanded it to do. It was to be fruitful, and this fruit was for our sustenance. Jesus saw it wasn't obeying the command of Father God and passed judgment on it, which is something that should be considered in-depth, apart from our present study. However, I thought it interesting enough to insert it here. There was a lesson to be taught that our Lord Jesus, through His actions, would instruct us in. It is worth mentioning as well; Jesus didn't say anything about it as He passed the tree. This is a fact we should observe attentively. More often than not, instruction takes place when someone seeks knowledge about a matter. And, the deep things of God must be searched out if we would know of them! Peter spoke to Jesus first, then instruction came! Think about this!

Peter commented on what took place with the fig tree. So, Jesus begins a simple yet profound teaching. Remember, Jesus, the Son of God; the Vine is pouring forth wisdom here. Let's see what He has to say. Our Lord Jesus made a simple reply to Peter. He said, *"Have faith in God."* This is the beginning of our Lord's counsel! The first thing is, *"Have Faith in God."* I will present something to you now for your consideration. Have Faith in God, your being in God, and God being in you! If you are indeed in Christ Jesus, you belong to God, and you are in Him. Have Faith in His counsel, which resides in you as you abide in Him. Have Faith that our Heavenly Father is directing you as He said He would, according to His Word. Have Faith that He is The Almighty God and that He is Alive in you because of Jesus Christ and His work upon Calvary. Again, this is the first thing, *"Have Faith in God."*

The next thing for us to consider is our position. We covered this briefly in Chapter 3 of this book. Remember that our *"Position or Posture of Prayer"* is in the Love of God, recognizing that we are His beloved children and that we come to Him as His sons and daughters through Jesus Christ, our Lord! As sons and daughters of Father God, we listen for His Word regarding our situation, then as our Lord Jesus did here, we declare His Word regarding the matter before us whatever it may be. Here the example was a fig tree that was not producing fruit as it indicated it should. There are a number of things we could examine about this very thing, though it may be best to consider it only in passing. For instance, the fig tree wasn't producing fruit, which could represent the unfruitful things in our own lives that we are given authority in the Spirit to demolish. The fig tree had signs of life! It had leaves. However, though the leaves were present, there was no substance. Fruitfulness is in Christ alone. Otherwise, all we exhibit is external fluff. Should we not speak what our God is speaking regarding these matters in our lives that we might become truly fruitful?

Since the first thing is to *"have Faith in God,"* and the next is to remember who we are in Christ Jesus our Lord, what is after this?

I believe after we have examined the first two things, we are to carefully reflect where we are in relation to our position with others. This teaching gives us an insight into what could be hindering our prayers before God. Jesus reminds the disciples to recall how He taught them to pray. This teaching ends in like manner. We are to make certain we are not harboring unforgiveness in our hearts. In other words, if we are unmerciful, or unforgiving, Father God will not forgive us. This is rebellion. God says we are to forgive, and if we refuse, we are rebellious towards Him. Why is this important? It is extremely crucial since Jesus places great emphasis on this as a requirement for standing in faith with God! Some may not see it this way. However, if this was insignificant regarding obtaining the answer to our petitions, before our Heavenly Father, Jesus would've stopped at verse 24. He did not! Therefore, it was given so that we might understand that faith in God is related to our present condition of fellowship with Him.

It may appear some are overcomers in this, and others that are not. However, I think it is important that we look to God. Jesus didn't say have faith in God as you see others having faith. He directs us to personally have faith in God. Don't look at what others around you have or don't have. We are foolish if we measure ourselves by other people. We are to measure ourselves by the Living Word of God and seek to follow after our Lord and His ways with our whole hearts. If we do, and we are walking in unbroken fellowship with God, our Father, and our Lord Jesus Christ, we will have the petitions we have asked of Him. This is His Promise! He will do what He said He would do. It may not happen suddenly, or perhaps it already has in the Spirit, and we just have to wait patiently for the manifestation of it. It may also be that God is forming in us a tenacious heart so we will not faint until the promise He has given becomes evidenced! Yes, in this instance, that fig tree died. However, what we don't often see is that it died that very moment. It was only the next morning that

Peter could see what had already been decreed by Jesus evidenced. Likewise, it may be the same as we are praying. We agree with our God and believe in our hearts for the thing we are praying about. We know for certain we are in fellowship with our Father, and we are resting upon, believing in Father God regarding a matter, that it will be as we have said before Him. We believe in our hearts with full assurance that it is a done thing. Now comes the waiting part! In faith, the matter is already settled in God. We know by the Spirit and not with our flesh, that we have prayed according to the will of God. We are in fellowship with Him. So, when will it take place? It already has! Now we wait for the fig tree to die if you will! Wait, and don't lose heart. You will reap if you faint not! You will reap if you faint not!!!! I didn't make a mistake in repeating this statement. Jesus wanted us to know that God will give us the desire of our heart as we pray in agreement that His Kingdom and His will is to be established in the matter. We speak what God is speaking, and we wait for the promise of our God to come forth in the name of Jesus!

Daniel prayed, and God answered him, but the answer didn't come to him in a second. However, it did come, and it was told him that the moment he prayed, God sent the answer (Daniel 10:12). So, the moment we pray, our Father in Heaven is gloriously moving on our behalf as His Beloved Children. Do we believe this? Lord, help us to grasp it now!

So, what do we do if we have been guilty of falling short in disbelief? The answer is "REPENT." Let's deal with the spirit of unbelief even as our Lord dealt with the fig tree. Cursed be that spirit which would defame our Heavenly Father and our Lord Jesus Christ! That unholy spirit must depart in Jesus' Holy Name! It is time to repent and stand up in God and send this foul demon to the pit in chains. We aren't to allow a spirit of self-pity and shame to take residence either. Let's repent and thank God for His mercy and bless His Holy Name, walking in fellowship with Him and speak what our Father is declaring over us. God is faithful! Let us no longer dishonor Him through our unbelief! When in doubt, run to Father God! Seek His Face! He will come and save! This is His Promise (Isaiah 35:4, Jeremiah 29:13, Matthew 7:7, Hebrews 7:25).

We are continuing to contemplate the *"Promises of Prayer."* Jesus gives us clarity about fellowship with our Heavenly Father through prayer. Again, Jesus the Living Word of God tells us that when we pray, we are to believe that we will receive what we are asking for. Because, with God, it is a done thing!

Consider for a moment the following passage of Scripture found in (James 5:16):

> *v16 Confess your faults one to another, and pray one for another, that ye may be healed. The effectual fervent prayer of a righteous man availeth much.*

See the first and the last part of this verse. Look at the results that take place as we walk in obedience to our Lord's command to *"love one another."* I say this is in love! Why? Because this is how we remain in fellowship with God. Here we see brethren confessing to each other their faults. This actually means to acknowledge our sins, our trespasses. However, it doesn't stop there. We are also instructed to pray for one another the effectual fervent prayer of faith in love! Observe how this measures with what our Lord Jesus was teaching. Let there be no bitterness or envy in our midst, but in love, serve one another. Love covers a multitude of sins. If we are willing to repent, then God will heal! He will heal us spiritually, physically, and emotionally. We are to be those who are willing, for Christ's sake, to forgive and to be instruments of healing to our brothers and sisters in Christ. I wonder how many people in the household of faith have been crippled because we have been unwilling, and unyielding before God, to forgive and pray for one another.

Let's reflect upon what Job faced a moment! His friends were not much comfort to him. On the contrary, instead of walking with him through the trial he was experiencing in love, they accused him of sin. Ponder this; Job didn't receive healing in his body until he prayed for his friends! By the way, his friends needed his prayers too. Why? They needed Job's prayers because God told them He wouldn't respect their prayers, but He would respect Job's prayers! Job was instrumental in their healing, and his, because he was willing to pray for his friends, who for some time didn't walk as friends. They received healing restoration to fellowship with God because of Job's willingness to intercede on their behalf. Likewise, Job obtained his deliverance because of this same willingness. I personally believe that when Job prayed for his friends, he did so as he prayed for his children! He asked God for mercy over them, even if they unknowingly committed sins. He was earnest with God, petitioning on their behalf like he would have someone pray for him.

I've included this example so that we might understand the importance of praying for one another in love. God will answer our petitions when they are clothed in His Love! God isn't a respecter of men's persons. However, God is a respecter of His Holy Word. Our Lord Jesus didn't present something to us that is out of reach. He doesn't tease us with a promise that only some can obtain! This isn't the heart of our Heavenly Father! It is The Father's good pleasure to give us the Kingdom! Likewise, it is His joy to answer our petitions. Recall once more, the Scripture found in Romans 8:32:

> *v32 He that spared not his own Son, but delivered him up for us all, how shall he not with him also freely give us all things?*

Dwell in this for a season! May this sink into our souls! With Christ Jesus, our Blessed Saviour, Father God will freely give us all things! Why? Because He Loves us! He proved it! We love Him too and seek to do those things which please Him. We don't do what He asks because He forces us to. Rather, we do them because we are filled with love and gratitude for all He has done for us. We keep His Word fresh and alive in our hearts because we love Him! We renew our minds because we want to be in fellowship with Him and know Him! Our Father pours out His bounty because He loves, and we receive of His bounty through prayer because He delights in answering us. So, don't lose heart! He will answer the cry of your heart, give you greater desires and answer them too!

There are a great number of promises written within the pages of the Holy Word of God. However, they are like the grapes on a vine. You can't distill the wine unless you crush the grape to get the juice. My wife shared with me that if we don't gather the grapes, they dry up like raisins. That's food for thought also! People who pray, stay in the right way, and if we don't pray, we will decay! If we don't pluck the grapes and crush out the juice, we might just find the grapes have turned to raisins! The Word of our Lord Jesus is drink indeed. But, it is impossible to enjoy the richness of this holy wine unless you press in to obtain it. Oh, how much richness there is awaiting which our Lord has prepared for our refreshing. See, now, if it is possible to number the gracious promises of our God! He is Eternal! So, can we number them out? Selah!

Let His Word now fill our hearts with joyful songs. He will answer when we call! Blessed be His Holy Name! Amen!

Dwell much here before we move on to the next insight regarding prayer, which is, *"the Peace of Prayer."* Praise The Lord Jesus!

CHAPTER 7
The Peace of Prayer

In this chapter, we will consider the *"Peace of Prayer."* As we contemplate this topic, may our hearts be in remembrance of the things our Lord revealed to us through the pages of this book thus far. Please understand there is a great deal more we can mine regarding prayer through studying the Holy Word of God, The Living Word! This study is meant to draw us closer and move us deeper into Christ. My prayer is that we will grow in Christ and in holy desire for Him and His Holy Word, as we continue daily seeking His Lovely Face!

Heavenly Father, we now come asking you for your Holy wisdom and counsel as we examine the *"Peace of Prayer."* Let the Holy seed of your Word come forth in the lovely Name of Jesus Christ. Let fruit spring forth even now, which will glorify your Holy Name. For, you are worthy, Most Holy God. I bless your Name, and thank you for the honor of sharing your Word with my brothers and sisters. Now, let your Holy Spirit breathe in us, filling us with your love and power, that we might increase in the knowledge of you and Jesus Christ, your Holy Son! Heavenly Father, we desire to increase in your Kingdom Power and Authority, in and through love for one another. Grant these things now I humbly pray in the blessed Holy Name of Jesus Christ our Lord and Saviour! Amen and Amen!

Holy Spirit, grant now your grace that I might have somewhat to impart to my brothers and sisters in Christ. Cause me to see and hear that which is in the heart of our Lord Jesus. I welcome you here! Be glorified through this book, Holy God, as I declare your precious Word! Amen!

As we begin this chapter, we should remember where our journey started and what it is our Lord desires for us. Prayer isn't a vain exercise! It isn't foolish repetition! Prayer is communing with God, our Father, and our Lord Jesus Christ that we might understand His heart and establish His Kingdom and Will in the earth, through that which we have heard!

Before we study the *"Peace of Prayer,"* I believe that we should consider the following *"Promise of Prayer"* found in Isaiah 40:21-31:

> *v21 Have ye not known? have ye not heard? hath it not been told you from the beginning? have ye not understood from the foundations of the earth?*
>
> *v22 It is he that sitteth upon the circle of the earth, and the inhabitants thereof are as grasshoppers; that stretcheth out the heavens as a curtain, and spreadeth them out as a tent to dwell in:*
>
> *v23 That bringeth the princes to nothing; he maketh the judges of the earth as vanity.*
>
> *v24 Yea, they shall not be planted; yea, they shall not be sown: yea, their stock shall not take root in the earth: and he shall also blow upon them, and they shall wither, and the whirlwind shall take them away as stubble.*
>
> *v25 To whom then will ye liken me, or shall I be equal? saith the Holy One.*
>
> *v26 Lift up your eyes on high, and behold who hath created these things, that bringeth out their host by*

number: he calleth them all by names by the greatness of his might, for that he is strong in power; not one faileth.

v27 Why sayest thou, O Jacob, and speakest, O Israel, My way is hid from the Lord, and my judgment is passed over from my God?

v28 Hast thou not known? hast thou not heard, that the everlasting God, the Lord, the Creator of the ends of the earth, fainteth not, neither is weary? there is no searching of his understanding.

v29 He giveth power to the faint; and to them that have no might he increaseth strength.

v30 Even the youths shall faint and be weary, and the young men shall utterly fall:

v31 But they that wait upon the Lord shall renew their strength; they shall mount up with wings as eagles; they shall run, and not be weary; and they shall walk, and not faint.

The promises of God are yes and amen, and here is one of them. Look at verse 31 for a moment! What a bountiful promise this is! Our Lord will renew our strength as we wait upon Him. He gives strength to run and to walk. Chapter 40 is a word that Isaiah was given after he prophesied of Israel's going into captivity to Hezekiah. This tells us of the redemptive work of our Lord Jesus. The *"Promise of Prayer"* here is the fact that our God will not leave us in captivity. Yet, while we are being buffeted about, He will come and give us His Holy Power as we wait upon Him! Our Lord doesn't leave us when trials become severe. *"He gives power to the faint; and to them that have no might He increases strength."* This comes as we wait upon the Lord our God! So, what does waiting look like? And, what does it mean when He says He will give us power and strength? Examine this text in the Hebrew, and we see what is promised to those who wait upon The Lord! See the

Strong's Concordance to understand the word *"wait"*:

> *OT:6960 qavah (kaw-vaw'); a primitive root; to bind together (perhaps by twisting), i.e., collect; (figuratively) to expect:*

> *KJV - gather (together), look, patiently, tarry, wait (for, on, upon).*

This is taken from the *Strong's Concordance*. Here we see that the word *"wait"* means to bind together (perhaps by twisting), i.e., collect; (figuratively) to expect.

Look at the phrase *"bind together"*! What can we glean from this? I believe this represents coming under the covenant of God, binding ourselves, wrapping ourselves up in Christ. In other words, *"Put on Christ,"* as the Apostle Paul wrote (Galatians 3:27). It is also doing so with an assurance that our Lord will fulfill His Word! Because, as we wait in covenant before our Lord Jesus, we also expect His promise to come! He will finish His holy work in and through us. Expect that it will come forth, have faith in God!

So, what is to be expected? The answer is power and strength. Let's examine this for a moment. *"He gives power to the faint..."* We will look at what it means to be faint and what it means to receive power. The *Strong's Concordance* defines faint as:

> *OT:3287ya`eph (yaw-afe';) from OT:3286; fatigued; figuratively, exhausted:*

Power is the word *"koach"* from the *Strong's Concordance*:

> *OT:3581 koach (ko'-akh); or (Dan. 11:6) kowach (ko'-akh); from an unused root meaning to be firm; vigor, literally (force, in a good or a bad sense) or figuratively (capacity, means, produce); also (from its hardiness) a large lizard: -ability, able, chameleon, force, fruits, might, power (-ful), strength, substance, wealth.*

To be faint means to be completely exhausted, and God has promised to give *"Power"* to the faint. Look at the fullness of this word! There is vigor, force, capacity, might, strength, wealth, just to name a few attributes. We need to realize that The Almighty God is the One who is giving us of His strength. It is from Him we receive power when we become exhausted, at the end of our rope, if you will. God will not leave us there. However, this promise is given as we *"wait"* upon our Lord as we bind ourselves up in Him. He will give us His power to do His will in the fullest sense of the word!

What about the second part? *"to them that have no might He increases strength."* Consider what is written here. There are moments when we have no might at all. This actually means to be completely spent, no power, no resource, absolutely nothing left! We have come to the end of ourselves and our resources, but this isn't the end of the story! Again, it is The Almighty God who gives us of His strength! This word is different than the one we just examined.

See the following from the *Strong's Concordance*:

OT:6109 otsmah (ots-maw'); feminine of OT:6108; powerfulness; by extension, numerousness:

KJV - abundance, strength

Once again, consider the fullness of this word. It is in Christ Jesus, our Lord, that we can do all things. This abundance is promised to us as we *"wait"* upon The Lord our God!! Looking carefully at the definition, we see the word *"powerfulness."* This sounds like an overabundance of strength, a spilling over because of the bounty given. This is superabounding in Christ, or we might better say, *"It is Christ in me..."* (Colossians 1:27). Jesus Christ, our Lord, moves by the Holy Spirit in and through us, on our behalf, fulfilling His Word, His promise to us! While we *"wait"* with expectancy upon our Lord, putting on Christ, His strength is imparted to us! Praise His Holy Name!

Remember, this is written to encourage each one of us to go deeper in Christ through prayer and study and be renewed in Jesus' Holy Name!

Our faithful God will finish His work in us. The passage of Scripture we just studied tells us that even when we are facing great trials, our God will give us of His power and His strength to walk in victory and not faint, to run with purpose and not grow weary in well-doing. This is His promise, and His Word will never fail!

The *"Promises of Prayer"* are many, and the *"Peace of Prayer"* is the assurance we have, knowing He is our God, and as we wait upon Him, we are renewed!

As I considered the previous passage in Isaiah, my heart was led to the place of mercy we have with our Lord. The peace *of* God and peace *with* God is at the mercy seat of heaven. We are studying *"prayer,"* and now we examine the *"Peace of Prayer."* This is why I believe The Holy Spirit led me to the *"Mercy Seat."* It is at the mercy seat that we commune with our Heavenly Father, and this is what prayer is! We commune with our Heavenly Father through the *"blood of the everlasting covenant"* (Hebrews 13:20), in Christ Jesus, our Lord! Here, in prayer at the mercy seat, all that we have need of is freely given. There is peace at the mercy seat!

We find one mention of the *"Mercy Seat"* in Exodus 25:20-22:

> *v20 And the cherubims shall stretch forth their wings on high, covering the mercy seat with their wings, and their faces shall look one to another; toward the mercy seat shall the faces of the cherubims be.*

> *v21 And thou shalt put the mercy seat above upon the ark; and in the ark thou shalt put the testimony that I shall give thee.*

> *v22 And there I will meet with thee, and I will commune*

with thee from above the mercy seat, from between the two cherubims which are upon the ark of the testimony, of all things which I will give thee in commandment unto the children of Israel.

The Hebrew word for *"Mercy Seat"* means to cover, to expiate. It is at the mercy seat that we find peace with God through the blood of Jesus Christ, which was shed for us. His holy blood was sprinkled upon the mercy seat of heaven, and now, through His precious holy blood, we can come boldly into the throne room of grace to find mercy and grace to help in times of need (Hebrews 4:16). Oh, how we need Jesus moment by moment. We can't do anything without Him, but all things are possible with Him! Hallelujah! Note in verse 22; the Lord God says, *"and there I will meet with thee, and I will commune with thee from above the mercy seat..."*. What a promise this is! Now we can commune with our Heavenly Father, and He has promised to meet with us there! I meet with my Father in prayer through the great mercies He has imparted to me in Jesus Christ, our Lord! He communes with us, and we commune with Him! What a wondrous blessing! This leads us back to the very beginning regarding the *"Purpose of Prayer."* We commune with our Heavenly Father so that we might understand His heart and then proclaim it in the earth. We are here to glorify His Holy Name. We seek His Kingdom and His Will. The *"Peace of Prayer"* is the assurance that God will indeed fulfill His Word. It shall come to pass. At the mercy seat we find atonement was made that we might come into the throne room of grace. *"Pardon for sin and a peace that endureth...*[3]*"*; praise His Holy Name, His Mercy Endures Forever (See Psalm 103)!

There is one more thing I would like to mention. Let's look at verse 21 for a moment. There is a nugget here to enjoy. We see that

---

[3] *Great Is Thy Faithfulness,* song written by Thomas Chisolm (1923), composed by William M. Runyan

the mercy seat is placed upon the ark of the covenant, which contains the testimony that God gave Moses.

What can we understand from this? We can see that access to the promises of God are through the blood! All the promises are underneath the mercy seat of heaven. There was no access to the promises of God without going *through* the blood. It is the blood of Jesus Christ that cleanses us, and through His holy blood, all the promises of God are freely given to us. His mercies, which endure forever, are through the blood of Christ. We are invited to come and drink of the fountain of Life, and this Life is in Jesus Christ, our Lord. The *"Peace of Prayer,"* as we wait upon God, is the assurance that we have obtained mercy through the blood of Jesus Christ, our Lord. His blood is the *"blood of the everlasting covenant,"* which is forever settled in heaven. Thanks be to God our Father that He provided us The Way, and it is in and through Christ Jesus our Lord!

Consider the following verse found in Numbers 7:89:

> *v89 And when Moses was gone into the tabernacle of the congregation to speak with him, then he heard the voice of one speaking unto him from off the mercy seat that was upon the ark of testimony, from between the two cherubims: and he spake unto him.*

After the dedication of the altar, which was sprinkled with blood, the LORD communed with Moses just as He said He would. The Promise that God made to Moses in Exodus 25:22 was fulfilled in this verse. Everything was set in place according to the pattern that God ordained. All things were made ready, as God instructed Moses to establish. The blood was sprinkled upon the altar, according to The Word of the LORD. Now, Moses could approach the mercy seat with full assurance that The LORD GOD would meet with him and commune with him there. It was as the ALMIGHTY said!

This access into the very throne room of our Heavenly Father, who Is The Almighty God, has been granted us through the blood of Jesus Christ, our Lord! We need not fear that God will not meet with us, nor will He fail to speak with us. We are instructed to come to the throne of grace boldly (Hebrews 4:16). This speaks of the work of Jesus Christ, our High Priest! Here, before our Lord, we can speak with our Heavenly Father with the full assurance that He will hear our cry. Yet, there is more! Not only will He listen to our hearts cry, but He will answer! The promise we are given in Hebrews 4:16 is that we will *obtain mercy and find grace to help in the time of need.* Moses did not have to be afraid to come to God. However, he did have to go through the blood of the covenant to stand in the presence of The LORD! Likewise, we need not fear coming to God, our Father. We come through the *"blood of the everlasting covenant,"* the holy blood of Jesus! Through Jesus Christ, our Lord, we can boldly approach our Father, who is waiting to hear our petitions and with joy, grant our requests while we wait expectantly before Him!

So then, may our prayers be offered with a heart full of thanksgiving and faith. Jesus said our God would answer speedily, as was revealed in Luke 18. So, may we run to our Heavenly Father and ask. Let the prayers of our heart be sincere and full of grace, knowing that our faithful Father will hear and commune with us at the altar of His grace! What should we expect to hear from our loving Father? I believe He will declare His Son, the Living Word to us. He will reveal to us the glorious promises written upon His heart, which are now available to us through Jesus Christ and revealed by the Holy Spirit.

The *"Peace of Prayer"* is at the *"Mercy Seat"* of heaven. Through the Precious Blood of Jesus Christ, we now have peace with God! This holy peace is what our hearts yearn for. Our Heavenly Father opens His arms with joy to receive us. He sings and dances over us because of what was accomplished at the Cross of Jesus on our behalf. We have peace with God, and we are free to come to Him! There is no need to wonder if God will accept us if we are in Christ! We don't need to wish that He would hear our prayers. He hears even before we cry out and He bottles up our tears! This is the peace we have been given through Jesus Christ, our Lord! Hallelujah! *"The blood of Jesus Christ avails for me, and His holy Word prevails for me.[4]"*

I join with the heavenly hosts actively praising my Heavenly Father and our Lord Jesus Christ! My communing with Him is so I may know His heart, that my heart may agree with His, establishing His kingdom and will be in the earth even as it is in heaven. I wait with joy and thanksgiving, binding myself to my Lord, for His Word to be fulfilled even as He said. For His promises are sure, and His Word is true.

We will see the things that our Lord decreed come to pass. But for the moment, we are to rejoice in the process. Even as the fig tree died the moment Jesus cursed it, the promises of God are being established! It will not be long before we see the coming of our Lord. It will not be long before the prayers that we have offered before our Heavenly Father are manifest. It will not be long before the victory that we have already been given is realized before our eyes. *"We do not look at the things which are seen but at the things which are not seen"* (Hebrews 11:1). The things which are seen are temporal. So, we set our eyes upon the Living Word of God, which is forever established in the heavens! Our weapons are not carnal. We do not fight in the flesh! Our weaponry is the armor of The Almighty God (Ephesians 6:11). Even when it appears that God hasn't answered our prayer, we are commanded to pray again in faith even as Elijah did (1 Kings 18:42-44). Elijah didn't see his prayer answered the first time he knelt to pray, though he was on his face beseeching God to bring rain. He didn't even see it

---

[4] Quote From: *Fortitude - A Necessary Possession*, Chapter 2 Page 12, by Robert L. Martin, Copyright 2017

manifest the second, third, fourth, fifth, or sixth time. However, the seventh time he offered his supplication to God, the answer was seen as a cloud in the sky the size of a man's hand. Now, it hadn't started raining yet! But, that little cloud was enough to let Elijah know God was bringing the rain. Elijah wasn't praying amiss. He offered holy prayer, and he didn't stop until he received the thing he asked for. So, keep asking, keep seeking, and keep knocking for God isn't finished yet. The answer is on the way.

Consider Daniel, he prayed for an answer to something that was troubling his heart, and God heard his prayer. The answer was sent the very moment Daniel set his heart to seek God (Daniel 9:23). However, the manifestation of that answer wasn't realized until he had been in prayer and fasting for 21 days. The answer is on the way already for those of you who have been seeking God about a matter. So, don't lose heart, don't faint! You will reap if you faint not! Hold Fast!

Personally, I have come to realize that some of the things I've prayed for and about God already answered! Yet, I continued to ask for them because I didn't recognize that He had already given me the answer to my petitions. We are required to walk the answer out with the faith of His promise. For instance, if we pray, *"Oh Lord be with me today,"* are we really asking aright? Did not Jesus say that He would never leave us nor forsake us? Rather, shouldn't we be seeking His counsel for the moment and offer Him thanksgiving for it? Please understand, I am not condemning anyone for earnestly praying for the Lord to be with them. As a matter of fact, the moment we begin to lift our prayers up to God in earnest, He is present. How can we be sure of this? Well, the answer is, we are praying! Prayer is communion with God The Father, God the Son, and God the Holy Ghost. So, when we lift our hearts to God in prayer, He is there. Here's a promise (Isaiah 65:24): *"...before they call, I will answer; And while they are yet speaking, I will hear."* Our prayers are not offered to a deaf God; neither are they offered to someone who can't hear us because He's too far away. The supplications we bring are to the Living God! He is Ever Present! And, Jesus our Lord is Ever Interceding for us. So, even if you can't feel His presence, just breathe His Holy Name! He's right there with you. Salvation took place when we came to God through faith in Christ Jesus. We asked our Lord to forgive us of our sins and cleanse us through His blood. Our hearts responded to His call in faith, and we believed that Jesus forgave us when we ran to Him. He still forgives, though we fall short of His glory. However, I've found myself asking Jesus to forgive me for things I received forgiveness for when I first came to Him. The Lord corrected me and said, *"I already forgave you; why are you asking about this again?"* I felt at that moment, the Holy Spirit saying that the enemy of my soul was bringing an accusation without cause. I am forgiven! The blood of Jesus avails eternally for me. Jesus already atoned for my sins and cleansed me. So, that kind of prayer is a prayer of unbelief. Remember, you were purged and walk now in the Light of that Word! I realized this was an issue with many of the prayers I had offered. I had asked in faith and then thought that maybe something was wrong with me, and God wouldn't answer. Please understand, there are things that will hinder our prayers. However, the Holy Spirit was saying to me that I needed to consider carefully *what* I was praying. He will convict me of sin if I am in error because I am following my Lord with my whole being. If we are in fellowship with our Lord Jesus and have assurance by the Holy Spirit that we are, then ask with faith in God! He will hear and answer at the Mercy Seat! He will commune with us there! Amen!

The invitation is given! Come to the Mercy Seat! Here our God will commune with us at the table of blessing! We will partake of the Manna, the Water, the Wine, and the Oil, which our Lord has prepared for us. The communion of our Lord is filled with the fragrance and sweetness of His Presence. Praise His Holy Name! Come to the table and partake. Taste and see that the Lord our God is indeed good beyond all measure. He offers us life today. Come now and receive it. Amen and Amen!!

Again, there is a great deal more that I could write about here. However, this book was written as a guide to encourage us to go deeper in Christ Jesus our Lord. Search out the Promises of God for they are indeed, Yes and Amen.

CHAPTER 8
The Practicality of Prayer

We come now to the final chapter of this book, which is the *"Practicality of Prayer."* It is wonderful to grow in the knowledge of our Lord and Saviour Jesus Christ. Truly, this should be something we desire to do as His beloved children. The Holy Spirit has given us many wonderful nuggets of truth through our study. Now we will seek the counsel of our Lord Jesus in the *"Practicality of Prayer"* and how we walk these truths out!

Oh, blessed Holy Spirit, we ask for your divine counsel! Open the eyes of our understanding and fill us with your Word and Will to walk out the truths you have given us. Make these truths alive in us that we might glorify our Lord Jesus. We ask these things in the lovely name of Jesus Christ our, Lord! Amen.

We are seeking to learn how to walk in the Spirit and apply these truths. God's Word is powerful and will change our lives if we allow Jesus to fill us. It is through His Word that we obtain victory! So, we need to begin by seeing what *"Practicality"* is.

The definition of "practicality" is the quality or state of being practical.[5] So, in our case, it is being practical about prayer. Remember, we said that prayer is not one-sided! It is communion with God The Father, God The Son and God The Holy Ghost. We are to walk in a practical manner regarding prayer, communing

---

[5] oxforddictionary.com

with God. To do this, we listen, talk, and listen some more! Then we walk out what we have been hearing while still actively listening, asking, seeking and knocking. Again, we seek to establish the Kingdom and Will of God in the earth through our prayers. The Father's Will is manifest through private *and* corporate prayers as we join our hearts with our Lord Jesus. Jesus walked before The Father in this way and gave us an example so that we might learn how to exercise our hearts in prayer. He perfectly lived out God's plan for His life because He was in constant communion with Father God! This is why we are instructed to, *"Pray without ceasing"* (1 Thessalonians 5:17).

My wife and I took a trip recently. During this time, our Lord Jesus began to reveal some things to us about the practical ways we serve Him. He revealed what is right with some things and what is an error. I believe it is important to relate them here since we are speaking of *"The Practicality of Prayer."*

Our trip was a blessing, though I was experiencing a health issue. I ended up in the hospital because of a spike in my blood pressure, which was due to pain from a severe sinus infection that was confirmed to us later on. It was during this time when I wasn't feeling very well, that my Lord talked with me about "getting on the same page with Him." While I was dealing with things in the hospital, and afterward during some sleepless moments, I heard my Lord speaking. It comforted my heart, even though I was in pain. The Holy Spirit gently opened my understanding of the practical walk of prayer. And, I was actually functioning in it at the time. It was as natural as speaking to you right now. He instructed me that this would be the closing chapter of this book. So, I will relate to you these things, and I pray we will all be filled anew with the Holy Spirit, who will enable us to work this out.

The first thing the Holy Spirit spoke to me was…"Get on the same page with God." I contemplated this while seeking the Lord for His counsel. He directed me to Colossians 4:6:

> *v6 Let your speech be alway with grace, seasoned with salt, that ye may know how ye ought to answer every man.*

God's divine influence in our lives enriches us to walk out His Will. This is grace multiplied towards us. And, as God has given this grace, we are to season others likewise. We are the salt of the earth, for so it is written in Matthew 5:13. This being the case, we are to bring the seasoning which God has poured out upon us to others. The seasoning is the work of Christ Jesus in us wrought by the Holy Spirit. He is the seasoning in our lives. Without this spice, we have nothing to offer those around us.

Practically speaking, to get on the same page with God is to say what He is saying. This requires the communion of prayer! If we are prayer-less, we have no seasoning to offer. Through communion, we hear The Father declare His Will. Then, we can speak what He reveals to us, giving an answer to those with questions.

The second thing the Holy Spirit revealed was..."Learn to speak what your Father in heaven is speaking, instead of the first thing that you think." This goes along with what was just revealed. We can't afford to be careless with our words! I was called to repent for speaking carelessly about issues I was facing. You see, there are words that are from God and words that are not! If we speak carelessly, we can be assured that careless things follow. Please understand, I am not a proponent of the "name it and claim it movement" of days gone by. For example, I want that fine car, that fine house or that great job. Consider the operative word in this type of prayer, "I." It isn't that we can't have these things or pray for them. After all, Jesus said we would receive them. Rather, we are to seek God's Kingdom and Will first. My earnest desire, however, is to speak what the Holy Spirit gives me to say. The Scripture I was led to regarding this matter is John 6:63:

v63 It is the spirit that quickeneth; the flesh profiteth nothing: the words that I speak unto you, they are spirit, and they are life.

Consider what Jesus is saying here. It is the Holy Spirit that quickens and gives life. The Holy Spirit is the seasoning that enables us to speak what is true and righteous. Jesus tells us that the Words He speaks are Spirit and Life. They are from God The Father, and they are for Life. There is no death in them. To explain more fully, there are no careless words in God. Jesus was careful to speak what God gave Him to proclaim. Jesus didn't say what others expected Him to say. He didn't speak what He thought was best! See John 12:49-50 for confirmation:

v49 For I have not spoken of myself; but the Father which sent me, he gave me a commandment, what I should say, and what I should speak.

v50 And I know that his commandment is life everlasting: whatsoever I speak therefore, even as the Father said unto me, so I speak.

And John 14:24:

v24 He that loveth me not keepeth not my sayings: and the word which ye hear is not mine, but the Father's which sent me.

Getting on the same page with God and speaking what He is saying, instead of what we think at first, is doing the Will of The Father. It is walking in unity with our Lord so that His Will is accomplished. Again, this is what our Lord Jesus did. See John 5:30.

v30 I can of mine own self do nothing: as I hear, I judge: and my judgment is just; because I seek not mine own will, but the will of the Father which hath sent me.

Since Jesus sought the Will of The Father and we are His beloved Body and Bride, should we not be doing the same? This is why we should be in constant prayer and communion with our Lord!

The Holy Spirit revealed to me that we declare and demonstrate the Love that God has for people as we walk out communion in this way. The Holy Spirit enables us to live out what is revealed, as Jesus did (Colossians 1:27)! *"Christ in us, the hope of glory."* We display the majesty of our Lord through obediently living in the Spirit, being in constant communion with our Lord!

The third and final thing the Lord spoke to me about was intercession. This book is about prayer, and such a conclusion is a fit one. Intercession is the deepest form of prayer! It is standing in the gap for others. Moses stood in the gap for the children of Israel at a time when the Lord God would have destroyed them because they rebelled against Him while Moses was on the mountain. See Exodus 32.

Intercession pleads for the Will of God to be accomplished and stands in the gap until it is brought forth in faith. Jesus was often in prayer seeking the Will of The Father. He would spend all night praying before ministering the next day. He is also our Great High Priest ever interceding for us before The Father (Romans 8:34 and Hebrews 11:25). Again, I submit to you, if Jesus Christ is interceding for us, should we not be those who stand in the gap for others?

The Holy Spirit helps our infirmities through intercession with groanings that are, at times, unutterable. See Romans 8:26-27:

> *v26 Likewise the Spirit also helpeth our infirmities: for we know not what we should pray for as we ought: but the Spirit itself maketh intercession for us with groanings which cannot be uttered.*

v27 And he that searcheth the hearts knoweth what is the mind of the Spirit, because he maketh intercession for the saints according to the will of God.

Intercession is the means to attain an object or an end. This is what the Holy Spirit is doing when He is before The Father for us, and He does so, "according to the Will of God." If we would have victory in prayer over circumstances that we face, it is through interceding for the Will of God. The Holy Spirit does this, for He knows the mind of The Father. He is the third Person of the Godhead and is One with God. He is the Spirit of our Lord in us! He will not pray counter to the Will of Father God. For, just as Jesus sought to do the Will of The Father, so also does the Holy Spirit. If we want victory over the battles we are facing, it will come through our yielding to the Holy Spirit. He will intercede on our behalf for The Father's Will to be established, that we might overcome according to His Will. This is why God The Father sent Jesus Christ His Son!

Jesus came that we might have a more abundant life. This doesn't mean having all the fine things of this world. Otherwise, Jesus would have made it perfectly clear that we were to have great earthly treasures. The abundant life is a life full of the love of God, knowing we are His, and we have been redeemed to God by the blood of Jesus Christ, that we might have eternal fellowship with our Father. The abundant life is also having a renewed mind, not a poor mentality, even if we are poor in this world. God never intended that we live with a faithless attitude towards life in any fashion. Yet, we are to live in complete submission to our Father, and this can only be done as we yield all that we are to Jesus Christ by following the leading of the Holy Spirit.

So, may the Holy Spirit lead us deeper as I share what was revealed to me specifically about intercession.

It is vitally important to understand that intercession is a critical part of obtaining victory in battle. If we do not have an understanding of the enemy we are fighting, it is certain the battle will be a costly one. We might win the war, but with pain and sorrow that could have been averted through intercession.

What is intercession? We spoke of this earlier. Intercession is seeking the Will of God about a situation, receiving His mind concerning it, then proclaiming His Word over the matter. We stand in faith, agreeing with God The Father, God The Son and God The Holy Ghost! God will reveal through intercession His Will. In turn, we proclaim His Will by faith. In other words, we see by faith what God is saying, and we speak it!

Intercession is also learning to cut off things in the Spirit. If something is spoken carelessly and the Holy Spirit checks us on it, cut it off by speaking the truth. This way, the lie is severed and cannot take root. If, however, we are careless with speech and give no attention to what we speak, that thing will grow. It will become a weed that is harder to deal with, spreading all over our field. God's garden requires careful and watchful keeping. Weeds grow easily. You don't have to plant them. They just show up. However, delicate flowers and beautiful gardenscapes must be cultivated and tended. Our heart is the garden place of our lives, and, too often, through neglect or lack of understanding, we allow weeds to enter. We must learn to be watchful over the things we speak. Cut off what is not of God, even if what you see is overwhelming to you. Go in the Spirit to God The Father in Jesus' Name and ask for revelation regarding your trial. He will reveal Himself *and* His Will to you!

As we discussed earlier, prayer is communion with God so that we might establish His Kingdom and His Will in the earth. So, intercession is pressing in earnestly that we might establish God's Will through His Word! In the Spirit, it is also binding and loosing according to His purpose.

Let's talk about binding and loosing a moment. The passage of Scripture we will examine is found in Matthew 16:19:

> *v19 And I will give unto thee the keys of the kingdom of heaven: and whatsoever thou shalt bind on earth shall be bound in heaven: and whatsoever thou shalt loose on earth shall be loosed in heaven.*

We see here that keys have been given, which are the *"keys of the kingdom of heaven."* Jesus was revealing to Peter and His disciples how they would establish The Father's Will. Jesus said he would give us the "keys." What are the keys used for? Keys are used to lock and unlock things. Here Jesus reveals these are keys that will lock things up according to God's Will, and they will open them as well. Jesus further declared that with these *"keys of the kingdom"* His disciples could bind things on the earth and they would be bound in heaven. What does this mean? Well, the word *"bind"* used in this passage from the Greek is the word *"deo."* It literally means to bind or tie up. Through this we understand that in Christ Jesus there is authority to bind, lock up, what is coming against us as we come into agreement with God's Will for His Kingdom on earth. What does it mean to agree? It is to be harmonious, to accord, or stipulate by compact (See Matthew 18:18-20).

I have witnessed people binding and loosing things that I knew in the Spirit was not according to the Will of God, which means it was not in agreement with our Covenant Deed in God through Jesus Christ. The results were ineffectual. Why? The answer is, the prayer did not agree with the Spirit of God regarding the situation at hand. The problem was a real problem, but everyone was so focused on the problem, looking for relief from the situation, that they didn't hear from God about it. They just tried the Word of God, instead of hearing from Him regarding His Word for the matter at hand. Listen carefully; God wants us to know what it is we *are* joined to and what we *should be* joined to. It is truly a holy compact (written decree) with our Father. Either we are in covenant with our Lord or something else! Likewise, I have heard some trying to loose things without obtaining victory. Again, because the prayer wasn't in agreement with the Will of God, it was something a person wanted for themselves. This isn't faith intercession. It is a careless prayer. I don't mean to offend, because I have been guilty of the same thing. However, as I have grown in Christ, I have come to know that true intercession is always with the Kingdom of God and His Will in mind, even in the smallest of things. God does want to bless us! However, Jesus said we were to seek the Kingdom of God first. His ways should always be first!

What about loosing? The word in Greek is *"luo."* It figuratively means to loosen. It can also mean, to break up or destroy. Jesus makes a statement to a woman who was bound with a spirit of affliction for eighteen years in Luke 13:11-13:

> *v11 And, behold, there was a woman which had a spirit of infirmity eighteen years, and was bowed together, and could in no wise lift up herself.*

> *v12 And when Jesus saw her, he called her to him, and said unto her,* **Woman, thou art loosed from thine infirmity.**

> *v13 And he laid his hands on her: and immediately she was made straight, and glorified God.*

He said to this woman that she was *"loosed"* from her infirmity. It is the Greek word *"apoluo,"* which means to be fully free. It is a compound word from *"apo,"* meaning off or away and *"luo,"* which is interpreted as loosened. Jesus made null and void the compact that was written against this woman. The compound word used can also mean to pardon, or specifically divorce, according to the *Strong's Concordance.* It can be understood by this that a decree had been written against this woman, and Jesus destroyed that decree. He made a new decree, a new covenant with her. It was a covenant of mercy and love; an exchange took place. A new decree was given because Jesus had the authority to make this covenant with her. In like manner, Jesus has all authority, and all power, which by His own Word has been given to us as keys to break off, destroy these enemies.

Let's look at the practical way we should bind and loose. To start with, since loose means to loosen, break up, or destroy, we understand it is about destroying the kingdom of darkness. So, with the keys of the Kingdom of Heaven in our hands, and through the discerning word of the Spirit of God, we loose, break up or destroy what is standing against God's Will. It is destroying the decree which the enemy has used to withstand God's people.

Notice the word *"keys."* It is a plural word, not a singular one. Why? It is that we might know there's more than one key and that each individual key has a specific purpose. For example, we don't start a car with a house key. You can't unlock the deadbolt on the front door with your office key unless they are all keyed the same. It just doesn't work. Likewise, there are keys to the Kingdom of heaven, and each key has a specific function. If you are going to enter a battle, you should know what's in your armory and what enemy you are facing. What does he have in his arsenal? In 2 Corinthians 10:4 Paul says:

> *v4 (For the weapons of our warfare are not carnal, but mighty through God to the pulling down of strong holds;)*

Notice Paul uses a plural word for weapons. Intercession is seeking God for His Will regarding our situation; obtaining by the Spirit the key to loose, destroy the enemy's hold of the thing, and bind our enemy so he can no longer function. Jesus said with these **keys,** we would be given authority to bind things in the earthly realm, and as they are bound in the earth, they are bound in heaven. So, by the revealed Word of God we bind or tie up our enemy from any further influence, and when it is bound according to the Will of God in the earth, it shall be bound in heaven. We also have keys to loose or cut off the work of the enemy in the earth and in our lives by the Spirit of God. When we do so, according to the Will of God, Jesus said this would be loosed in heaven, the spiritual realm. The second part of this is binding ourselves to Jesus Christ, wrapping ourselves up in Him, and sending forth His Word over the things we are facing. The Lord is the One who fights for us. If we would win the battle it must be in and through Him! We can't defeat the enemy of our souls without Jesus Christ. However, we do overcome by His blood and His Word! Again, intercession in the Spirit is seeking God for His Will regarding the situation and obtaining the key to execute His Will in the earth over it. This is walking in God's governing authority, bringing His government into being, *"on earth as it is in heaven."*

The understanding of binding and loosing is a necessary part of our intercession. Now that we have counsel about this, I have something else to share with you. It is about intercession on a corporate level.

The Holy Spirit revealed this to me as I was praying over things relating to the Body of Christ, both locally and around the world. He said the Church of Jesus Christ would not obtain great victory without great intercession. This means the Body of Christ must come together and seek the face of God for the keys necessary to bind and loose the things that are actively hindering the Body of Christ, and it must be done in the spirit of unity, according to His Will. We must be willing to gather and pray for one purpose, to glorify God in the earth. Let us learn to listen that we might hear what God is saying. Then we must be bold to declare His Word as He reveals it, binding what needs to be bound and loosing what needs to be loosed so that the Body of Christ will grow in strength, instead of becoming weak and frail.

I believe another matter should be addressed, which is very significant. It is the matter of being filled up. When we have obtained an answer from God through prayer, it is a great moment of rejoicing, and well it should be. However, at times, the rejoicing over that victory ceases as we progress forward on our journey. If the victory was a great deliverance, we need a great filling in its place. We also need to place a marker, a stone of remembrance there. How? By recalling the victory that praise may spring forth once more. If our Lord answers our prayers and we fail to bring praise and set up our *"stone of remembrance,"* then, what may follow through our indifference is carelessness before God. Indifference is a deadly enemy; it invites worse bondage than was ours previously. So, raise up holy praise for what God does and mark that place where God delivered. When the storm comes, and the winds blow, we will recall what God has done thus far, knowing He will lead us onward. For, *"hitherto hath the Lord helped us"* (1 Samuel 7:12).

The Holy Spirit continued to give clarity to intercession. He said you must have at least three who will intercede, and three offices need to be exercised. He said there must be Priestly Intercession, Prophetic Intercession, and Kingly Intercession. In each successful victory, these three will be represented. Why? They represent the Godhead through intercession.

What is the Priestly intercession? It is the prayer that deals with the condition of the people before Father God. This interceding breaks the bondage of sin that may be hindering the move of God. The Priestly Intercession moves in the Spirit as Christ intercedes for His Bride before The Father. Likewise, this prayer will seek to behold the Bride of Christ perfected. It will always seek the unity of the Body of Christ as our Lord Jesus Himself sought. See John 17. This Priestly Intercessor will, by the Holy Spirit, seek to establish the Body of Christ in righteousness and truth, renouncing all sin, bringing reconciliation to the body.

What is Prophetic Intercession? Prophetic Intercession, like Priestly Intercession, is led by the Spirit of God. The Prophetic

Intercession continues before the throne of God, waiting for the counsel of The Father to be released over a particular situation. As The Father reveals His Will and Mind by the Holy Spirit, the Prophetic Intercessor begins to proclaim God's Word and Will to the heavens. This intercessor will declare the counsel of God and through prophetic utterance, in the Holy Spirit, will bind and loose strongholds, proclaiming God's victory.

What is Kingly Intercession? This is intercession that has heard the mind of The Father through prophetic intercession and seeks the equipping to establish what has been decreed by God in the Spirit. This intercessor obtains counsel from God and prepares the army for battle, establishing the strategies for successful warfare, through the leading of the Holy Spirit. The Kingly Intercessor proclaims the authority of the King of Kings so that the Kingdom of God may be established in the earth and in the church's sphere of influence.

Each type of intercession can be exercised by an individual because we are children of the Most High God. When we move in the Spirit, God The Father (Kingly) , God the Son (Priestly), and God the Holy Ghost (Prophetic) will exercise in us this intercession. However, we were not made to be islands. If we would have great victory, it will be through great corporate intercession.

There is a Scripture regarding this in the Old Testament. One can put a thousand to flight, but two can put ten thousand to flight (Deuteronomy 32:30). What can three or more do? Selah. The witness of this type of intercession in the Old Testament is found in Exodus Chapter 17. It reads:

> v10 So Joshua did as Moses had said to him, and fought with Amalek: and Moses, Aaron, and Hur went up to the top of the hill.
>
> v11 And it came to pass, when Moses held up his hand,

that Israel prevailed: and when he let down his hand, Amalek prevailed.

v12 But Moses' hands were heavy; and they took a stone, and put it under him, and he sat thereon; and Aaron and Hur stayed up his hands, the one on the one side, and the other on the other side; and his hands were steady until the going down of the sun.

v13 And Joshua discomfited Amalek and his people with the edge of the sword.

Notice there were three necessary for Joshua's success. The Priestly Intercessor was Aaron. He saw Moses needed help, and he joined himself to Moses and brought along Hur. This was intercession that brought unity. The Prophetic Intercessor was Moses, for he declared the Will of God. He raised his hands for what Jehovah promised was theirs. This was the intercession of victory. The Kingly Intercessor was Hur. He sees that victory is assured when Moses keeps his hands raised. So, joining with Aaron, they get a rock for Moses to sit upon and hold his hands up until victory was accomplished. This was a strategic intercession, which reveals the practical part of prayer. Hur was of tribe of Judah, which also represents victory through praise. However, that is an entirely different subject for another time.

This picture was also represented in the reign of David. He was the Kingly Intercessor. Nathan was the Prophetic Intercessor, and Abiathar was the Priestly Intercessor. It is written in 2 Cor. 13:1:

v1 ...In the mouth of two or three witnesses shall every word be established.

Each person can function in one or more of these offices. Why? Because the Holy Spirit imparts the anointing for the office. So, when two come together in agreement regarding a situation, the Holy Spirit will direct the prayers upward and the answer down, as we humbly pray. The verse above tells us a minimum of two is necessary. However, as in Joshua's case, three were needed to see complete victory, and I believe this is what the Holy Spirit was declaring to me when He said three were necessary for a great victory. As it is written in Eccl 4:12:

> v12 And if one prevail against him, two shall withstand him; and a threefold cord is not quickly broken.

A rope with three strands tightens together under pressure and doesn't easily break. So, it is able to withstand the pressure and perform a task that a single strand cord cannot. Likewise, when the Priestly, Prophetic, and Kingly intercession joins together, the prayers offered are prevailing prayers, which bring forth victories that would not otherwise take place. Similarly, "A house divided cannot stand" (see Matthew 12:25, Mark 3:24,25, Luke 11:17,18). If a house is divided about anything, that division will bring forth destruction. Why? First, because our Lord Jesus proclaimed it, and His Word is the Truth! Second, God is not the author of confusion. The Spirit of God will not come and abide when a spirit of division is in our midst. He doesn't push Himself upon anyone. However, He will urge us to draw together in Christ. We are the ones who are required to lay aside differences and obey His leading. The Spirit of The Living God will abide when our hearts seek to abide in Christ. In our Lord Jesus Christ, there will always be unity and liberty. Where Jesus truly dwells, no accusation can abide. We may hear the loving rebuke of our Lord as we enter into His presence. But, this is for our admonition, to bring us closer into fellowship with Him. Our Lord, through the Holy Spirit, doesn't rail upon one of His children, though He may firmly correct. This is always done in His lovingkindness. In these instances, the Body of Christ comes together addressing any sins present and then moves from this to thankful praise and worship for the correction received. Thus, the Holy Spirit will lead us into deeper communion with our Lord, which will give strength and counsel to move forward in Christ.

There is one final point to make regarding *"The Practicality of Prayer."* It is the matter of the Cross of Jesus Christ. All true prayer flows from our experience at the foot of the Cross! Indeed, everything worthwhile in our lives has its beginning at the Cross. If we have not been to Calvary, we do not know Christ, and our prayers are futile, except for the prayer of salvation there. Our prayer, our communion, and our very lives as children of God flow from the Cross of Jesus Christ. On the Cross, the precious Lamb of God gave His life for us that we might be delivered from death. All who receive Jesus Christ, at the foot of the Cross, receive life eternal. Prayers made which flow from the Cross of Christ are life-giving prayers. Words offered from this place of peace bring forth life.

What should we understand about our relationship with our Lord Jesus from this place? Paul gives the answer to this question when writing to the Corinthians. Consider the following words of 1 Cor 1:18-24:

> *v18 For the preaching of the cross is to them that perish foolishness; but unto us which are saved it is the power of God.*
>
> *v19 For it is written, I will destroy the wisdom of the wise, and will bring to nothing the understanding of the prudent.*
>
> *v20 Where is the wise? where is the scribe? where is the disputer of this world? hath not God made foolish the wisdom of this world?*
>
> *v21 For after that in the wisdom of God the world by wisdom knew not God, it pleased God by the foolishness of preaching to save them that believe.*
>
> *v22 For the Jews require a sign, and the Greeks seek after wisdom:*

v23 But we preach Christ crucified, unto the Jews a stumblingblock, and unto the Greeks foolishness;

v24 But unto them which are called, both Jews and Greeks, Christ the power of God, and the wisdom of God.

If we would understand our salvation, it is in the Cross. Paul tells us in verse 18 that *"preaching the cross"* sounds foolish to those who are lost. It just doesn't sound *"logical."* After all, don't we need to do something to be acceptable to God? The answer is; We can't do anything! Our ways, thoughts, and deeds are not acceptable to God unless they come through the Cross of Jesus Christ. He is the only acceptable gift. The Greek word used for *"preaching"* in this text is *"logos."* It is the Word of the Cross of Christ that Paul says is the *"Power of God"*! It is not our efforts or our gifting! It is the "preaching of the cross."

If we would examine the verses following this, we might understand why the *"preaching of the cross"* was chosen by God to be the instrument of power towards us. We tend to puff ourselves up through knowledge. However, God's ways are higher than ours! According to verse 21, worldly wisdom tends to turn us away from God. When a person thinks he knows everything, you can't teach them anything! The Jews were looking for signs and could not see the signs in front of them because of their intellectual pride. The Greeks were seeking for some higher wisdom so they might be like God themselves. They couldn't see because the wisdom men possess apart from God is utter foolishness. For God is the Eternal God. Our Father chose to use something base and ignoble to confound man's wisdom. Paul declared that Christ crucified is the wisdom God used to bring eternal life! It's not our labors or our intellect that makes us acceptable to God and offers life. It is the Cross of Jesus Christ alone! In Christ alone, there is the power to Save, Heal and Deliver!

Our labor must flow from the Cross. For, this is *"Christ the*

Power of God and the Wisdom of God"! The reason is found in verse 29 of this same chapter. It is so "that no flesh should glory in His presence." It is Christ in us the hope of glory, not our personal achievements that make us acceptable to Father God (Colossians 1:27). It pleases our Heavenly Father when we receive His Holy Son as the atonement for our sins (Isaiah 53:10). This is true because God's greatest gift to mankind was and is His Son! If we refuse Jesus Christ and His atonement upon the Cross, we refuse God's greatest love gift. And, if we reject The Father's supreme gift, we reject the gift of eternal life. Eternal life is only in Christ Jesus, our Lord, The Father's perfect gift!

The Cross is the final Word over all things in the most practical sense. It is our beginning in Christ, and from there, our fellowship continues and flourishes until the day our Lord comes again for us! Until then, I pray that in some way, you are strengthened and encouraged as you read this book.

For those of you who do not know Jesus Christ as your Lord and Saviour, I offer you this humble prayer. Oh Lord Jesus, I come to you as I am. I need a Saviour, for I am a sinner. You said that if I come to you, confess my sins and ask you to forgive me and cleanse me; you will receive me. So, Lord Jesus, I confess my sins to you and ask you to make me whole. Wash me in your blood and cleanse me from my sins. I ask you to be my Lord and Saviour right now, and I receive your forgiveness. Jesus, come and live in me and fill me with your Holy Spirit even now. I believe you are the Lord and I thank you for making me yours forever. Amen!

If you made this your prayer, welcome to the family of God. Now, ask the Lord to direct you to a church body that will love and strengthen you in your new walk with Jesus. Continue in your walk by prayer and study of His Word and Jesus will come and reveal Himself to you by His Spirit.

To anyone who desires to be made whole again, I pray the

Holy Spirit quicken you in the Mighty Name of Jesus Christ! Holy Father, let your love and grace envelop your beloved ones even now. Jesus, imprint upon this heart your Word of Truth! Holy Spirit, reveal this Truth to them even now. Even so, let it be done in the Name of The Father, The Son, and The Holy Ghost. Amen.

I leave the following blessing with each one of you. The Lord said to place His Name upon His people in this way, and He would bless them. It is my hope and prayer that you would truly be blessed and strengthened as this is offered to God on your behalf. May the Spirit of the Living God quicken you according to His Holy Word. This is my embellishment of the blessing!

May the Lord God bless you and keep you, May He who Is, Was, and Is to come make His Face to shine upon you. May the Lord our God be gracious to you, lift up His Countenance upon you and give you His Holy Peace! Amen. (Numbers 6:24-26).

Visit GodsWordPrevails.org
for more articles and inspiration